CULTURE SHOCK!

*Living and
Working Abroad*

Monica Rabe

Graphic Arts Center Publishing Company
Portland, Oregon

In the same series

Australia	Israel	South Africa	London at Your Door
Bolivia	Italy	Spain	Rome at Your Door
Borneo	Japan	Sri Lanka	
Britain	Korea	Sweden	A Globe-Trotter's Guide
Canada	Laos	Switzerland	A Student's Guide
China	Malaysia	Syria	A Traveller's Medical Guide
Czech Republic	Mauritius	Taiwan	A Wife's Guide
Denmark	Morocco	Thailand	Working Holidays Abroad
France	Myanmar	Turkey	
Germany	Nepal	UAE	
Hong Kong	Norway	USA	
India	Pakistan	USA—The South	
Indonesia	Philippines	Vietnam	
Ireland	Singapore		

Illustrations by TRIGG

This book is published by special
arrangement with Times Editions Pte Ltd
Times Centre, 1 New Industrial Road, Singapore 536196
International Standard Book Number 1-55868-304-6
Library of Congress Catalog Number 96-77214
Graphic Arts Center Publishing Company
P.O. Box 10306 • Portland, Oregon 97210 • (503) 226-2402

Printed in Singapore

To Olle and Johan Fredrik Gustaf and Carin, with whom I have shared so much excitement challenge and joy.

To Barbro, for putting me on the right tracks.
And to life.

CONTENTS

A Note From the Author   6
Introduction   9

   1 Culture – A Definition   12
   2 Getting Prepared   19
   3 Moving Out   28
   4 Your New Home   38
   5 The Outside World   51
   6 Culture Shock   59
   7 Language Barriers   65
   8 Communication   70
   9 Schools   76
10 Single Life   86
11 Staying Together   93
12 Working Life   104
13 Social Life   114
14 The Jekyll & Hyde Syndrome   123
15 Safety Abroad   127
16 Home Leave   134
17 Relocation and Repatriation   138

The Author   148
Index   149

A NOTE FROM THE AUTHOR

For your information, in particular to non-native English speakers, this book is written in easy British English and could be considered as a little exercise in the English language. The language is not difficult or complicated and should be easily understood by anyone with English as a second language contemplating accepting an assignment abroad.

If you have problems understanding this book I recommend that you quickly sign up for a class in English before leaving. English is truly the international language in which we can communicate all over the world.

In order to adjust quickly to a new culture, it is essential to be able to communicate with the host nationals primarily in English and, in nations with other languages, preferably in their native tongue as well.

However, remember that not until one masters the intercultural communication skilfully can it be said that one speaks any language fluently!

EXPATRIATE

The term 'expatriate' is applied to all persons working and living abroad, in other words a country that is not their own by citizenship.

The term can also be abbreviated 'expat' – a very common way of talking about foreign nationals.

Many people who hear this term for the first time wrongly believe that the word is expert. Although you might be an expert in the field you are being sent out for, it is not the right interpretation.

THE ACCOMPANYING SPOUSE

Throughout this book, the word 'spouse' is used instead of 'husband' or 'wife.' The reason is obvious – it is a neutral word and will not offend anyone engaged in the debate about equal rights.

The word 'spouse,' however, is usually the same as 'wife.' In spite of Women's Liberation and equal opportunity, there are still not as many women as men on foreign assignment. That time has yet to come. In most countries it still seems to be a man's world when discussing employment abroad.

The time has yet to come when it is common for a woman to ask her husband to take leave of absence from his job and accompany her on an assignment abroad. His duties will be then to take care of the household, the children and possibly the entertaining of business contacts.

Little did I know in 1987 when I started to write the first draft of this book, then called *Living Abroad – A New Insight* that it would lead to a new professional career within the intercultural field and yet another two books.

I would also have found it hard to believe, at that time, that I was to update the same book for the third time eight years later while living in Vietnam. When my first book was written I had only future Swedish expatriates in mind, but now, I want to reach anyone who is contemplating a foreign assignment. The questions that we ask ourselves are not limited to one nationality – they are universal.

In 1987 I led a busy life caring for my husband and our four children in Virginia Beach, USA and today I lead an active life together with my husband and our Labrador dog in Vietnam. Our children are spread all over the world studying and pursuing careers of their own.

In retrospect our lives form interesting patterns that almost appear carefully planned and masterminded. Our family's weave is a colourful multicultural blend filled with happiness and joy but also tears and sad goodbyes.

Living abroad involves experiencing new cultures, making new acquaintances and coming to a deeper insight about life and the world in which we live. Personally I will never regret our years in foreign countries even if it means living far away from our family and friends.

However, the thoughts of my loved ones are always there. I follow them closely and keep waiting for our next reunion filled with short, intense 'quality time.'

—Monica Rabe, Ho Chi Minh City, Vietnam January 1996

INTRODUCTION

Simply put, money is what makes the world go around. Economists call it 'the market' others call it 'greed' but one thing is for sure, money has a great attraction to most people, since money in fact also means freedom. In the pursuit of money many risk their lives, both physically and mentally. Money can lead some into dangerous adventures and others into risky ventures.

Whether it is the attraction of 'gold' or the pure global adventure that make expatriates choose a lifestyle which means moving from one country to another is a hypothetical question. The fact remains that quite a number of people have opted for this type of living. Many expatriates say that their real motivation is the excitement and challenge they feel living in different cultures; that they have a desire to experience and learn as much as possible during a lifetime.

Many expatriates will always feel restless and unable to settle down in one place. Children trailing along have been named 'global nomads' not really aware of their cultural origin. This might be the price to be paid when changing countries and cultures frequently. Their roots will never reach down deep enough in the soil before it is time to break up and leave for new endeavours. This could be considered a 'water lily life' – an existence of floating on water. The cost could be a certain loss of national identity and feeling of belonging.

Our world is getting smaller through sophisticated communication. We are constantly updated about the world via the mass media and news reaches us within seconds. Most people take an active part in the international world affairs concerning the economy, politics or global environment. Companies must adapt to a diminishing world dominated by rapid change. They become more vulnerable due to inter-linked economies and markets while the world's industrial base is shifting to countries where inexpensive labour is offered.

International and multinational companies are to be found all over the world. Brand names do not necessarily lead to the country of origin but symbolise the core values of the products marketed and sold. The motto: 'Think globally but act locally' seems to catch on. Corporate cultures merge and join forces in spite of national differences. However, international business enterprises cannot survive without competent people who can work within a global market. High demands are placed on the international staff and their families who must be able to adapt to a lifestyle that might be far from what they were used to. Interaction with people from other cultures is an absolute necessity.

With an openness and interest in people and other cultures, you can reach far and enrich your life. To have the privilege of travelling and experiencing other countries by being a part of them is very rewarding. It is like reading an interesting book – some chapters are very dramatic and intense, while others just carry the story over to the next thrilling episode.

The opportunity to live, work and travel in different countries has given me an insight into other cultures and an opportunity to perceive that, although there are great differences between the nations of our world, we share many things. We are dependent upon one another and are basically very much alike. We all struggle for a kind of survival, whether it be in a developed country or a developing one. When it comes down to the basics in living, such as relationships between human beings, communication, awareness, self-perception, upbringing of children, schools and careers, we are very much the same.

The intention of my 'book of experience,' as I see it, is to share with future expatriates what I have learned, and I hope that it will be of help in making life easier and more enjoyable abroad.

Living in a foreign culture is like playing a game you have never played before. The rules have not been explained and it might be difficult to play, but the challenge is to enjoy the game without missing too much. Eventually you will learn the rules and develop skills as the game continues.

It is my wish that this book will help you to play the various games a little bit better. There are always rules to a game and this could perhaps be called a general description of the rules of the 'expat game.'

Chapter One

CULTURE – A DEFINITION

Most people symbolise culture with the arts – literature, painting, theatre, and opera for example, and refer to socially or intellectually cultured persons, well versed with refined manners.

Culture, however, is so much more. Culture refers to the total way of life of particular groups of people. It includes everything that a group of people thinks, says, does and makes – its customs, language, material artifacts and shared systems of attitudes, values and feelings. Culture is learned and inherited and passes from one generation to another. It is one of the controlling influences in the way we live, think, speak and behave. It definitely reflects a nation's business culture.

The inhabitants of a particular country share similar values and attitudes, as they have been subjected to a so-called 'enculturation' all their lives. This enculturation takes place initially within the families but in countries with politically strong programs it is also handled by politicians, efficient mass media and supportive educators. The educational system of a country indirectly or directly supported by religion or faith can help to preserve or change ideals, values, morals and accepted ways of behaving.

COMPARING CULTURES

By contrasting one's own culture with that of another country, we will soon discover that each country and thereby its culture is unique. It has formed the people living in its environment. In the attempt to discover one's own culture, there is a great opportunity to better understand one's own country and its people. The awareness and understanding of cultural identity will help you to understand and accept foreign cultures. Before knowing where you are you should know who you are. In attempting to do this we discover that many cultures share similar values and beliefs.

We have to remember that every culture is so-called ethnocentric, which means that it thinks its own solutions are superior and that it would be recognised as superior by any intelligent, logical person. Each culture's own view of the world is perceived as the most natural, common view of the world.

It is interesting to note here that a small tribe in New Guinea, for example, that many might consider primitive, does not consider their culture at all primitive. They have really never questioned themselves and lead a life that suits their particular needs.

Not until people from different cultures meet do we discover similarities and differences in the way we behave and associate with each other. In order to avoid significant culture clashes we must try to identify some commonly held values and from there on start building strong, long-lasting bridges. Cultural differences combined with national pride and superiority can destroy any good intentions of cooperation between countries and businesses alike.

The key to success is to be able to understand and accept different values and behaviour – and this we do if we try to learn the hidden and invisible foundations of a culture.

THE ICEBERG THEORY

A culture could well be likened to an iceberg. Any country's cultural iceberg consists of at least ten common denominators, all of which are the same but perceived differently. They are:

- Food
- Clothing
- Shelter
- Social organisation
- Government
- Defence
- Education
- Religion
- Family organisation
- Knowledge and science, including arts, culture and crafts.

From these denominators, of which education and religion are the most important, differences and similarities with our own culture can be judged. By analysing, understanding and comparing our own cultural baggage, or 'iceberg,' with other cultures, it will help us to broaden our multi-cultural knowledge and thus facilitate our adjustment to and cooperation with people from various cultures.

When visiting a country for the first time we see only the most apparent differences and similarities. We notice the top of the iceberg. This may be more or less visible. The greater the ethnic and geographical differences appear, the higher the top. This could mean that we are more prepared for difficulties and challenges when the top of the iceberg is clearly recognised.

If we, for example, compare countries within the Western or Asian regions we might not see the top of the iceberg as clearly. We think that our cultures are similar, which in fact is true, but the differences are greater than we believe and this in turn could lead to many unfortunate mistakes and misunderstandings.

■ ■ ■ ■ ■ ■ ■ ■ ■ ■ ■ ■ ■ ■ ■ ■ ■ ■

The First Impression of a Culture

	Smell	People	Clothes	Service	
Symbols	Sounds	Races	Dress Code	Bureaucracy	Architecture
Language	Food		Greetings	Corruption	Monuments
	Beverages				Roads, Streets
Mass media				Climate	Traffic
Communication				Nature	Pollution
				"Animal Life"	Population
Standard of living					

Norms and Values

■ ■ ■ ■ ■ ■ ■ ■ ■ ⊕ ■ ■ ■ ■ ■ ■ ■ ■

Key Consultants Inc. / M. Rabe

It is important to try to analyse what we find under the surface of the iceberg when trying to understand a new culture. Not until we start living in a new country on the same conditions as the inhabitants, will we discover the fundamental differences in attitudes, values and behaviour, in other words what lies in the invisible part of the iceberg – and it is here that the challenging learning process starts.

Not until we speak the 'multi-cultural language' can we fully adjust to a foreign culture.

A CULTURAL CHECKLIST

Below is a checklist for gathering basic factual information about your host country according to Dr. L. Robert Kohls book, *Survival Kit For Overseas Living*. It is not essential, however, that you follow the exact sequence given here. If you are vitally interested in a particular section, for example, start there.

Symbols

- Symbolism of flag
- National anthem
- National flower
- Myths and legends of different ethnic group(s)
- National holidays
- Traditional costumes

Human and Natural Resources

- Geography and topography
- Regional characteristics
- Major cities
- Natural resources (flora, fauna, minerals)
- Climate
- Demographic information
- Transportation systems
- Communication systems
- Mass communication media

Family and Social Structure

- Family structure and family life
- Family roles
- Social classes
- Social organisations
- Social welfare
- Customs (birth, marriage, death, etc.) and courtesies

Religion and Philosophy

- Religious beliefs (indigenous and borrowed)
- Philosophy
- Proverbs
- Superstitions

Education
- General Approach (e.g. rote memorisation vs. problem solving approach)
- School system
- Colleges and universities
- Vocational training

Fine Arts and Cultural Achievements
- Painting
- Sculpture
- Crafts
- Folk arts
- Architecture
- Dance
- Drama
- Literature, poetry
- Cinema

Economics and Industry
- Principal industries
- Exports/Imports
- Foreign investment
- Cottage industries (if any)
- Industrial development
- Modernisation (if applicable)
- Urban and Rural Conditions
- Agriculture (crops and animal husbandry)
- Fishing (if it is a major activity)
- Marketing systems

Politics and Government
- System of government

- Political parties
- Government organisation (national and local)
- Current political figures
- Police system
- Military

Science
- Inventions and achievements (throughout history)
- Science
- Medicine

Sports and Games
- Native sports (unique to the country)
- Modern world sports
- Traditional children's games

National Foods
- Ingredients
- Methods of preparation
- Rituals and taboos

National Language
- Origins of language
- Local dialects
- Influence of external languages

Chapter Two

GETTING PREPARED

An assignment abroad is not a prolonged vacation. This is serious business! Working in a foreign country places high demands on the working spouse as well as on all the accompanying family members. The decision to accept an international job offer must be preceded by a thorough discussion within the family where everybody feels responsible and part of the team – successful time abroad relies on teamwork. Taking this new step and moving into a new direction will influence the rest of your lives, not least the accompanying children who most likely will be educated in an international school system.

There are naturally many questions you should ask yourself before accepting this assignment. Below will follow the most important ones to take into consideration before making a final decision.

When a whole family moves abroad, it is of great importance to understand that the accompanying spouse and children are not just 'accompanying baggage,' but equally as important as the person who accepts the assignment. A family in harmony will make the stay successful. And successful international families will always remain close even if they may later end up living far apart.

WHY AN ASSIGNMENT ABROAD?

Career-wise you will of course ask yourself what this particular assignment will mean to you and your family in the future. There are always risks in leaving a good job. You may not get the same position back when you return, and you must not take for granted that your foreign experience will automatically lead to an advancement in your career in the home organisation. Your colleagues will continue to advance within the company, which is under constant development and change.

People tend to forget you while you are away if you do not remind them of your existence. It is therefore advisable to find a mentor or 'buddy' at home who will keep you updated regarding domestic developments and keep your interests in mind for the time you are due to return.

Goals and Needs

It is also important to be aware of one's goals in moving abroad. They can vary from career advancement to just wanting a new professional and personal challenge but they could also simply be a need to get away. Maybe the idea of making more money is attractive – or is it a pure desire for adventure? Whatever the motives, one must be aware of them because they play a great role in one's experience abroad and are important to the success of the stay in a foreign country. However, trying to escape from personal problems or difficulties in the relationship with your partner is not going to work. These problems will not disappear but instead become increasingly larger.

These goals and needs must be clearly understood by the whole family.

Your Spouse's Career

What will this assignment mean to your accompanying spouse's career? Is she/he willing to leave a good job, social security, and possibilities for advancement? Is she/he prepared to take a break in the professional career and perhaps risk not getting the position back upon the return home? Have you looked into the possibility of continuing dual careers in the new country? What is there to gain in coming along?

Accompanying Children

What do the children say? Are they prepared to leave friends and relatives (and sometimes pets) for a long period of time? Are they aware of the fact that they will have to start a new school career, make new friends and in many cases learn to master and compete in a foreign language? Remember that teenagers usually feel the breaking-up quite dramatic but that they also adjust very quickly to their new lifestyle and usually appreciate their new international school situation tremendously. They get a head start in our shrinking international world.

Stable Marriage/Relationship

Another crucial question to be raised has to do with the stability of one's marriage/relationship and family life. If there are any doubts, you should not even contemplate going abroad because a shaky relationship can never be improved by changing living conditions. There will be great demands on all of the family members, who will go through many rough seas together. The need for basic security within the family and between the two partners is of extreme importance to living in harmony and making the stay successful.

Parents/Grandparents

Some other concerns to be met are one's parents' situation in the case that they need care and help. Are there any problems you foresee in leaving them alone? What kind of practical arrangements must be made? Are there any sentimental bonds that might disturb the family later?

21

Health

Last but not least, it is essential to have good health. Can your family's health needs be met without any problem? Are there any chronic diseases or other physical conditions that cannot be taken care of abroad? Enquire about the medical services in the city and country in question.

REWARD

If you feel mentally prepared and ready to leave your basic security in exchange for a demanding, challenging and at times difficult life, you should accept the assignment abroad.

There is no doubt that the time spent abroad will influence all the family members' lives and sometimes even change their courses. The foreign experience will have a great impact on everyone's personal development.

Once happily back home again, you will be greatly rewarded through your memories of all the joys and discomforts that you have experienced together. A relationship usually becomes stronger after a successful period abroad and the family unit remains very solid.

Humour

A good sense of humour is a trait that everyone going abroad should possess. Many frustrating situations, at work and at home, will be eased by using the most effective weapon against hopelessness – the ability to laugh, shrug one's shoulders and see oneself from a different perspective.

IMPORTANT CHARACTERISTICS IN PERSONS STATIONED ABROAD

- Competent
- Tolerant and aware of one's own as well as the foreign culture

- Open and broad-minded
- Able to adjust
- Able to communicate and listen
- Stable and secure
- A good sense of humour
- Adventurous and curious
- Creative
- Good and sound relationships within the family
- Independent family members
- Good alcohol habits

The above characteristics are not necessarily placed here in order of importance. The type of work you do and the size of your family, for example, make some characteristics more important than others.

CHECKLIST

Family
- The spouse's work – Leave of absence
- Contact the children's schools. Arrange for transcripts or certificates
- Translation of school certificates
- Correspondence studies
- Inform relatives and friends
- Addresses and telephone numbers
- Arrange for pets

Home
- Rent or Sell
- Care of house and garden
- Cleaning
- Electricity, telephone etc.

Leisure
- Handling of boat, camper, car
- Resignation from associations
- Cancellation of newspapers, magazines, book clubs
- Union membership
- Planning for sports equipment to be available at the place of stationing
- Subscription of newspapers

Health
- Check Up
- Medical appointment (the whole family)
- Vaccinations
- First Aid Kit
- Medical kit (various prescriptions)
- Health certificate for Work Permit
- Dental checkup

Foreign Language
- Testing of language skills
- Language instruction (the whole family)

Internationalisation
- Pre-visit (husband and wife)
- Internationalisation seminar
- Research regarding the country and the place of stationing
- Films
- Meeting with a 'resource family' (former residents of the country)

Taxes and Income
- Tax Declaration
- Tax planning
- Taxation of real estate in other communities

Insurance
- Meeting with an insurance consultant
- Insurance abroad
- Home insurance
- Insurance of stored furniture etc.
- Evaluation of antiques, paintings, rugs etc.
- Photos/video of valuable household goods and furniture
- Insurance of house, car, boat etc.
- Other insurance
- Pension Insurance
- Pension plan/private and national
- Moving certificate

Other Activities
- Tax adjustments/final salary
- Bank accounts/domestic and abroad
- Company car

Private Economy
- Stocks and bonds
- Interest rates
- Property tax
- Bank savings
- Cash and travellers' cheques
- Credit cards

Traffic
- International Driver's License
- Foreign Driver's License
- Traffic rules
- Tax free cars / rules and regulations

Passports, Visas and Work Permits
- Valid passports during the whole stay
- Visas
- Work permit
- Residence permit (for the family)

Moving and Storage
- Moving the whole home
- Moving part of the home
- Moving of personal belongings
- Purchases
- Time for moving
- Means of transportation
- Formalities/ permits
- Customs and general regulations
- Inventory lists
- Inventory lists (storage)
- Insurance of stored goods
- Safety deposit box (bank)
- Sales tax exemption certificate
- Extra financial allowance

Notification of Moving
- Post office or local parish
- Local tax authorities
- Post office

- Telephone
- Electricity
- Sanitation
- Social Insurance Office
- Schools, daycare centres, play schools
- Military authorities
- Financial institutions /study grants etc.

DEPARTURE

- Itinerary
- Travel allowance
- Baggage/hand baggage
- Special hand baggage for the children (favourite toys, books etc.)
- Children's food

Chapter Three

MOVING OUT

When the decision has been made to 'take the plunge,' a very stressful period in your daily life will follow, culminating in the actual departure for the new country. Try to organise your activities and divide the different chores between family members. The checklist included here is an excellent help in keeping you up-to-date before your 'final countdown.'

FACT FINDING

The first step to take is talking with someone who has lived in the particular country to which you are moving. Maybe an arrangement can be made so that you will meet and interview your predecessors. Try to talk to different couples. You will find out that they all have different experiences to share with you. Ask questions and make notes. Try to find literature and travel guides from the country. Contact the embassy in question and ask for information. It is also advisable to watch films or read literature – short stories or novels – set in the area in question. Be curious and open-minded.

NEW LANGUAGE

As we said in the introduction, it is necessary for non-native English speakers to master English while living and working abroad. If you are to be confronted with a second foreign language, it will be of great help to find a short introduction to the particular language. A crash course a couple of months before departure will give you a good start in the new country. A phrase book introducing you to the alphabet, the numbers and common daily phrases will come in handy. The 'natural method' – listening, learning and imitating – will do wonders once you are settled in the host country.

English

For non-native English speakers, if English is the language of business or administration in the new country and your English needs to be brushed up, do not hesitate to take a quick refresher course. Start reading literature, newspapers and magazines in English and listen to all the TV programs in English without reading the subtitles (unless you live in a country where they have decided to dub all foreign movies).

NEW CULTURE

Every foreign country has its own culture which differs from our own. We find many common denominators in our own countries, but also a great many differences. When moving to a new country, with different culture and religions, it is important to read about this and be prepared to encounter all the many new facets. It is not necessary to be overly ambitious, but learning the basics will facilitate understanding peoples' actions and behaviour.

Naturally one will learn as one continues to live and work with the host nationals, but with a cultural awareness you will avoid many initial mistakes.

PAPER WORKS

If you are being posted, your company will of course help and advise its employees about all practical arrangements, such as insurance, work permits, visas, passports, birth certificates, driver's licenses and photos etc. (Refer back to the checklist in the previous chapter.)

It is advisable to make a list of all personal data, such as the numbers of credit cards, bank accounts, passports and visas, driver's license and car registration numbers – in other words, all pertinent data that might be needed if something is stolen or lost.

HEALTH

A physical examination of all family members is usually required by the company or the new employer. Medical questions will be brought up, various vaccinations given together with a general updating of everybody's immunisations. Certain countries require an HIV-test.

All family members should have their individual vaccination certificates, with the blood group stated in case a blood transfusion should be needed.

Special medicines and other medical aids should be taken along as well as prescriptions for eyeglasses. It is advisable to keep a private health card for each family member, as you will be much more in control of your own health care, changing and choosing your own doctors and hospitals. Dental records should be kept up-to-date. Find out if your children's teeth should continue to be treated with fluoride.

SCHOOL CERTIFICATES/TRANSCRIPTS

Make sure that all your children's transcripts are translated and updated. Ask a teacher to write a letter of recommendation regarding your child's social and academic development. Formalities are important in most countries.

If grades are not awarded in your school system until high school (which is the case in Sweden, for example) it is important to obtain from the school a general letter of introduction, together with a certificate regarding your children's academic and social standing. This certificate should be accompanied by an official letter from the school, duly signed and stamped.

Note that some schools do not accept children with handicaps or learning disabilities.

HOME LEAVE

The various practical arrangements to be made at home depend of course on the length of your assignment abroad. If your contract has been signed for at least three years, it will usually include a home leave every year. Your home has most likely been rented for the whole period of the stay abroad and a place will be needed for the annual return.

Especially when children are involved, it is ideal to return to a rented place close to your own home. A summer cottage is another good alternative, as the children can then return to their own rooms and their familiar things once a year. Hopefully their friends will be there waiting for them, too. It is very important for the whole family's well-being to maintain a feeling of belonging to the native country. The national identity will remain very important as time goes by and the children grow older.

WHAT TO BRING – PACKING AND MOVING

Planning ahead for a new future also includes starting to think of the practical details and what to bring to the new country.

Clothing

Depending on the climate, you must make provisions for the clothing you might need. In some countries it could be difficult to find the clothes you like or the sizes you need.

31

It is important to remember to pack some formal clothes, as there will often be some entertainment on behalf of your company and sometimes your country.

Different countries have different dress codes and it is important to check the local standards before stepping out in your regular attire.

Special Food

In countries with an existing expat colony, most of your needs will be looked after. Certain national foods that we feel we cannot live without, representing our roots and native culture will be missed as time goes by, and it is recommended to bring some of these specialties, in case they are hard to find, and enjoy them at times.

Newspapers and Magazines

In order to keep up with what is happening at home it is recommended to subscribe to a national weekly magazine and a daily paper unless you can easily obtain them in your new country. CNN and BBC World reach us even in the remotest corners of the world today, but it is always nice to have a national view of the news as well.

Furniture

Depending on the company's policy and the circumsatnces of your employment, you may be allowed to bring your furniture to some countries, while renting or using company-owned furniture is the arrangement in others.

Bringing your own furniture will give the best personal satisfaction in the long run – again especially with children in mind – as there is a certain security and identification in personal possessions, with memories and reminders of your background.

Small children should have their dearest toys and other special and familiar things around them in their new environment as they are not mature enough to accept too many sudden changes.

Special Things

As most of us moving abroad will become very nationalistic when certain holidays approach, it is important to bring all the traditional holiday decorations. Don't forget your cookbook with your favourite recipes. If moving the entire household is not permitted, it is advisable to take along decorative items, wall decorations, paintings, china, glasses, some rugs and linen. These familiar items will be appreciated once the family is settled in their new and foreign home.

Some practical things, such as 'fix-it-kits' and a good tool box, are handy; kitchen utensils, pots and pans are also great to have but can often be easily found in most countries.

Books for both children and adults, photo albums and maybe a recent film of relatives back home are other items to include.

Tapes or tape recordings from radio programs in your country or CD's with folk music in your own language, Christmas carols and other tapes representing your culture will be enjoyed at times while living abroad.

Children growing up in a foreign culture also need to be familiarised with their culture's traditional stories and fairy tales. Recordings of the most popular children's stories are wonderful, and so are children's movies as they represent part of their cultural heritage. They will also keep their native language active just by listening.

Souvenirs

One should not forget to bring some small gifts for people you will visit or to whom one might feel grateful, such as your children's teachers or sports coaches. A small, gift representing your country when visiting a person for the first time is always appreciated.

Students

A good dictionary together with a practical encyclopedia should be taken along. Families with school children will have especially great use of these books.

It is advisable to bring colour slides or a video film and a few good pamphlets about your country written in English as people most likely will show a great interest in your country, its history and political structure. The school children might be asked to write special reports on your nation. Try to bring informative 'fact sheets' on your country or a couple of good travel guides with colourful pictures.

Moving with Children

Remember that children could be extra sensitive when moving because it will lead to great changes in their lifestyle. It is important to keep the children involved in many of the practical details such as finding a home and choosing schools. The following points will help children to accept the mpve more readily.

- Give them information about their new country and their new school situation so that they know what to expect.
- Let small children pack their own boxes with toys, books and favourite things, and write their names on the boxes. Make sure they unpack the same boxes upon your arrival in the new country.
- Exchange addresses with friends at home and stay in contact with them during the period abroad.
- Pay close attention to the children during the first months in their new environment, keep all channels open, ask questions and give them good support and practical help. Share all their experiences and be aware of any changes in their attitudes or physical activities, such as sleeplessness or poor appetite. Approach the new situation with a positive attitude.

Storage of Furniture and Household Goods

When storing all or part of the furniture, it is of utmost importance that the storage company is reliable, professional and in good standing. A detailed list of all household articles must be made and photos must be taken of all valuables, such as paintings, rugs and silver, in case of

fire, theft or other loss. A couple of other points to remember:
- The insurance taken must cover the full value of one's possessions. Be particularly cautious with valuable art and antiques.
- Try to be present when your goods are being packed, and make sure that the container is sealed when leaving your home. Also be present when opening the same, witnessing the breaking of the seal.

Medical Kit

To countries with a less developed medical system one should bring a good first aid kit with medicines and other equipment that can be used in case of emergencies such as snake or insect bites, various allergic reactions or acute stomach disorders. In any of these cases, it is a great advantage to be able to help oneself until expert help can be obtained. Check with your doctor and get professional help.

Forwarding Address

Remember to let the rest of the world know that you are moving and remember to keep in touch with your friends and relatives.

An annual, lengthy, informative Christmas letter, perhaps with a photo of the family, will be greatly appreciated by everyone at home. It will also keep them updated about your experiences abroad.

ON YOUR MARK ... GET SET ... GO!

As you are ready to leave, go with an open mind and try to be positive and ready to face your new world. Be prepared to encounter difficulties and meet them with a good attitude.

Many choose, on their way to the final destination, to make a short stop over at some spot in between to catch their breath after a very hectic and stressful period. After a couple of good, relaxing days together, the family is better prepared psychologically to face their new life.

A NOTE TO YOUR DOG – TO GO OR NOT TO GO

Depending on how well liked and appreciated you are as a dog-member of the family, you might foresee an international life as well.

If the decision is to leave you at home, you will most likely be in good hands and can look forward to meeting your family every summer.

To be an accompanying dog, however, is most challenging and rewarding. You are together with your family and well treated as the good dog you are. You will feel at home quickly wherever you go with your family. There might be some problems culture-wise but you will overcome them and make new friends within a short time. Before you leave, see to it that you get a good health checkup and necessary vaccinations.

While the rest of the family will enjoy the comfort and luxury in the cabin of the aircraft, you are going to spend the trip in a relatively comfortable cage in 'cargo class.' The comforts of a tree, lamppost or other facilities are not available, no festive meal, few drinks and no movies. On the other hand, you might have interesting dog-passengers to bark with.

Most countries will permit you to come with your family, provided that all your papers are in order, but unfortunately, there are countries in the world that will not accept you right away on arrival.

Australia, for example, wants you to stay in quarantine for nine months, the state of Hawaii (but not the rest of the US) and Sweden for four months, while Great Britain has a time limit of six months. This is something to consider before you decide to leave. Your transportation and stay at the quarantine is also very costly.

Some Formalities Before Leaving

Find out what vaccinations and blood tests are required before entering the new country and investigate if there are any special procedures on arrival. Get your international health certificate updated, duly issued and stamped by an authorised veterinarian.

PRIVATE HEALTH CARD – AN EXAMPLE

Name: ....   Birth date: ....

Blood group: ....

Eye glasses: ....

Allergies: ....

Vaccinations:

Type: ....   Date: ....

Type: ....   Date: ....

Type: ....   Date: ....

Type: ....   Date: ....

Medical History:

Health Record:

Illness: ....   Date: ....   Medication: ....

Illness: ....   Date: ....   Medication: ....

Illness: ....   Date: ....   Medication: ....

Illness: ....   Date: ....   Medication: ....

Other Notes

37

Chapter Four

YOUR NEW HOME

FINDING YOUR NEW HOME

Unless you are the first person being sent out on a foreign assignment to a particular country, your new home is usually waiting for you upon arrival in the host country. People very often move into their predecessors' home, sometimes taking over pets and, in developing countries, also the domestic help which naturally will facilitate life considerably.

Professional Help

However, if you have to find your own home while on pre-visit or after arrival, you definitely should contact a relocation expert who usually cooperates with a realtor. They will lead you through the jungle of good and bad districts and be of great help. They are familiar with the local area and will assist you during your initial stay. You will be informed regarding rules and regulations and they will help you when signing contracts for a lease. Do not try to do this on your own. You might make many regrettable mistakes.

Location

If you bring school children along, they should be the decisive factor in choosing where to live. If there are many schools to choose from, it is important to find out from the local company and the people already stationed in the area where the best schools are to be found. A relocation agent will furnish you with all the necessary information regarding the various schools, their programs and academic standard. Quite frankly, the best schools are usually located in the better neighbourhoods. The school must have good resources, special programs for non-native speakers and thereby previous experience in taking care of foreign students.

Private or parochial schools could also be a good alternative. These are generally smaller and more familiar and can often take better responsibility for your children. Private schools are, however, very costly, not the least the larger international schools. Whatever you or your organisation decide, the closeness to school is vital, as many after-school activities take place there too, and it is a great strain to keep transporting the children daily, especially in congested traffic.

Other things to think of are that the house should be close to community facilities, hospitals, shopping areas and, in the best case, work. In any event, closeness to work must play a more minor role if you have your family with you.

Generally you will decide upon a home in an area where compatriots or the international community live, for many practical reasons. You will be able to share many daily chores, help each other with babysitting and support each other as you learn to live in a foreign country. The children will have friends to play with who speak the same language, which could be a relief after a hectic day in a foreign environment. This is particularly important in a Third World country where it is so much harder to integrate with the host culture and where a child's world is very restricted and isolated.

A FEW HINTS WHEN MOVING WITH CHILDREN

- Be positive about your new environment, as your children will be influenced by your attitude.

- Keep a normal family schedule and avoid too much extra stress which usually comes with change anyway.

- Organise your home quickly, and let the children decorate their rooms in a personal way.

- Get acquainted with your neighbours and try to find families with children.

- Bring your children to the school, meet all the personnel and make contact with a person (counsellor) whom your child can seek out in case of a problem.

- If your children need extra help with their school work, try to find a tutor right away.

- Discuss with your children all the activities at school as they need to share their experiences.

- Engage your children in sports or club activities. Do not be afraid of trying new ones. This will lead to new friendships.

- Look into the availability of carpools organised by the parents.

- Encourage your children to invite friends to your home.

- Plan 'discovery tours' in the new area with the whole family.

- Visit libraries, theatres, shopping centres etc. and try to develop a feeling of familiarity with the new environment.

- Try to be patient and open to all changes in your children's attitudes and behaviour. Remember that it takes much effort and time to grow new roots.

HOUSING IN A DEVELOPING COUNTRY

When choosing a home in a developing country, it is of course extremely important that you find a safe neighbourhood. Many choose to live in compounds surrounded by walls, consisting of a number of houses with common facilities such as tennis courts and swimming pools. They have fairly safe 'streets' to use for biking and jogging which is a relief if you live in a city with dangerous traffic and much criminal activity.

When looking for a home take the following facts into consideration:

- Flood risks
- Sanitation
- Water supply
- Security
- Utilities
- Electricity
- Heating and cooling systems
- Telephone
- Television (cable and broadcast)

Make a checklist and be careful to ensure that the house is in good condition and running order. Make certain that the house is considered safe and blessed by 'good spirits' – there might otherwise be problems finding domestic help.

Living in a Third World country involves certain restrictions of freedom for security reasons. Much time is spent inside the house and the garden, which is enclosed by high walls or fences. This in turn means that your living quarters should have ample space.

In a tropical country where the weather is very hot and humid, it is not essential to have a large garden as outside living is not that common.

Many seem to prefer air-conditioned rooms – at least bedrooms. After the initial suntanning euphoria, many prefer to stay out of the burning sun.

41

Also, you may experience a greater sense of insecurity in having large gardens, as it will involve a large area to guard and might attract intruders.

Electricity

Be particularly aware of the electric installations in the house if you live in a developing country. It is very common to get electric shocks when only changing a light bulb or switching on the lights. The children must be cautioned to be extremely careful when touching anything that has to do with electricity, such as outdoor lampposts, electric sockets, cords and plugs. It is not unusual that the plugs fall off, leaving an electric cord exposed. Many accidents have occurred because of poor workmanship.

Domestic Help in a Developing Country

If there is a possibility to take over the domestic staff employed by your predecessors do not hesitate to do this. They are usually English-speaking and familiar with the daily routines. In general, they are very loyal and trustworthy. When employing a new maid/servant, you must check his or her references, call the former employers if possible and make sure that their papers are in order. Try to find out the reasons for their having taken leave of their former employer. Be aware of problems like theft or dishonesty. You can also contact local agencies when hiring new staff. In many Asian countries Philippino maids are in high demand as they are very professional and skilled for domestic work.

As their employer, you must be in charge of the situation but refrain from becoming a fierce controller of their whereabouts. Your detergent and washing machine might be used, some leftover food will disappear at times – these are things one must accept. It is, however, important to let them understand that you are on top of the situation while 'looking through your fingers' – a technique one will learn as time goes by.

No one will benefit from over zealous control. On the other hand, you must never allow yourself to become too friendly and open with your household workers as this may embarrass them greatly due to the hierarchical structure often prevalent in their society. There must be a mutual respect for each other where you, as the employer, are in charge. It is important to be addressed by the family name or first name and Mr. or Mrs. or Miss. Your employees might also like to be called likewise.

Your family will become their social security and their bank, and form their large families' support. A close relationship will gradually start to grow as they become part of your private life. After a while you will be as dependent on them as they are on you. Having people working professionally in your home is sheer heaven for any family used to handling all the domestic work themselves.

Pay and Pay Respect

As far as pay is concerned, you must compare with the other expatriates already living in the area. Certain allowances must be included in the working conditions, but these vary from country to country. In general you pay an extra month's salary per year plus accumulate over the years an additional month's pay which you give them when terminating their contract.

A record of the names of the persons working for you together with their social security numbers or registration numbers should be kept and updated with an account of their weekly pay.

In these countries you must accept and respect the religious holidays, in particular their lunar calendar New Year. Give them time for worshipping and allow other rituals and beliefs.

Hygiene

Finally you must stress over and over again the importance of hygiene. It is important to teach all the persons employed by you to handle garbage properly, to watch out for flies, mosquitos and cockroaches that spread many diseases. They must be cautioned to keep control of rats and other animals. They must be aware of the link between sickness and poor hygiene. It is a matter of a long educational process where you generally are the expert. They will learn from you and become aware of these matters to their own benefit.

Health Checkups

It is generally a good idea to offer the domestic help an annual health checkup, including a TB control, as tuberculosis is a very common disease in Third World countries. It is also recommended to vaccinate all against typhoid and cholera, for example. Get some advice from your local doctor or medical association.

It goes without saying that you and your family also must have regular health checkup when living in developing countries. Pay more attention to your health and ask your doctor for advice as soon as you or your family members feel unwell.

Water

Drinking-water in many of the Third World countries should be boiled for at least 20 minutes. There are many other methods for making the water drinkable, such as applying ultraviolet light or using other water purification devices, which supposedly kill all bacteria. Be overly cautious when handling water since it contains many of the microorganisms that you must avoid in order to stay healthy. Teach your domestic staff to properly clean and dry all your kitchen utensils. Rinse all your vegetables in purified water. Remember that human waste is often used as fertiliser. Never use tap water – not even when brushing your teeth. When bathing children sterilise their baths as well.

Doctors do recommend drinking bottled spring water that also contains all the necessary minerals and salt that a human needs.

Cosy House

It is said that home is where the heart is, and making your home cosy and comfortable will make it easier to adjust to your new environment. It is in the home that everybody will find rest and a feeling of security when the outside world feels alien and threatening.

SOME COMMON TROPICAL DISEASES

AIDS (Acquired Immune Deficiency Syndrome)

This rapidly spreading disease must be mentioned on the list of tropical diseases since the HIV virus which eventually causes AIDS has spread rapidly in particular in developing countries. This is due to socioeconomic factors and poor education among the people. It is spread through hetero-and homosexual intercourse and via blood and blood products. Many carriers of the virus, such as prostitutes, might not be aware of the fact that they carry a deadly disease. There is no cure or vaccine for the disease.

Amoebic Dysentery

Amoebas are one-celled organisms which cause intestinal infection. It is transmitted through food such as salads not properly rinsed or contaminated water. The symptoms range from minor problems to severe diarrhoea. The infection can spread to the liver. It can be treated with antibiotics.

Cholera

This is a bacterial disease also spread via food and water. The symptoms are fever, vomiting and diarrhoea. There is a vaccine but it is fairly inefficient.

Dengue Fever

This is a viral infection spread by mosquitos. This disease is also called 'break-bone fever' with symptoms like severe pain in the muscles and joints. It can sometimes also cause bleeding in the skin and mucous membranes.

Dysentery

This is an intestinal disease caused by amoebas or bacteria. It is spread from human to human and via food and water the so called faecal-oral way. The symptoms consists of fever, stomach pain and diarrhoea. It can be treated with antibiotics.

Giardiasis

This is caused by a microorganism, Giardia, living in the small intestine. It is spread via faeces to water or raw food products. The symptoms are mild diarrhoea and a feeling of flatulence. It can be treated with antibiotics.

Hepatitis A, B and C

These are viral infections (infectious jaundice) which cause inflammation of the liver. The symptoms could be headache, nausea and body ache. Type A is much more serious than B. Hepatitis A is spread via faeces and Type B and C are transmitted via blood and sexual intercourse. Preventive measures are injection with gamma globulin every third month.

Hookworm Disease

Hookworms live in the small intestine and can cause anaemia. It can be spread via larvae penetrating the skin of the feet.

Japanese Encephalitis

This is a viral infection affecting the brain. There is a vaccine.

" JOHNNY AND SARAH CAN'T COME TO SCHOOL TODAY BECAUSE THEY'VE GOT ....

Leprosy

It is caused by bacteria often spread only after long contact with infected persons. It is a disease that destroys the nerves that control feeling and muscles. Treatment is available.

Malaria

This is a fever disease caused by the malaria parasite which is a microorganism spread by the bite of infected mosquitos. Signs of infection appear from 10 days to many months after an infected bite. Symptoms vary, from fever, chills and sweating to diarrhoea, bodyache and headache and if not treated properly it can lead to death. Unfortunately the malaria parasite has become resistant to many of the traditionally prescribed drugs, but there is intense medical research in process and new drugs are being tested presently.

Plague

This disease is a bacterial infection found among rats and spread via fleas to humans. There is a vaccine and treatment is with antibiotics.

Rabies

This viral, incurable and deadly disease is spread usually via bites and saliva from dogs, cats, raccoons and monkeys. Incubation period is generally 2 to 3 months. Rabies vaccination must follow within 48 hours together with immunoglobulin against the rabies virus to those who have not been vaccinated earlier followed by a series of vaccinations.

Salmonella

These infections are caused by bacteria which can be found in all kinds of meat, unpasteurised milk and powdered egg. Symptoms are vomiting, diarrhoea and sometimes fever. Antibiotics are generally avoided.

Schistosomiasis (Bilharzia)

This is a worm disease caught when swimming in fresh water and man-made lakes with infected, contaminated water infested with fresh water snails which are the carriers of the disease. The worms penetrate the skin and migrate in the body to the intestine. Treatment is available.

Sleeping Sickness

This is caused by a microorganism spread by biting bugs or tsetse-flies. The first symptoms are fever and swelling of the lymph nodes. There is no vaccine.

Toxoplasmosis

This disease is caused by a microorganism spread by cats (faeces). It can also be found in meat which is not properly cooked. The symptoms are hard to characterise. Pregnant women risk that the foetus also becomes infected causing severe damage to the child.

Tropical Sprue

A disease causing diarrhoea and weight loss. The reasons are unknown but it leads to malabsorption of many nutritional substances such as vitamin B12.

Tuberculosis

This is a very common disease caused by bacteria which can lead to infection of many organs, mostly to the lungs. It is spread by infected persons but also via unpasteurised milk of infected cows. Treatment is available.

Typhoid Fever or Paratyphoid fever

These diseases are caused by bacteria spread via faeces, urine or contaminated food and water. The symptoms are high fever and diarrhoea usually after a week. Treatment is with antibiotics.

Worm Diseases

The most common ones are roundworms, pinworms and whipworms – all spread faecal-orally. Medication is available.

Yellow Fever

A viral infection spread by mosquitos. The symptoms begin with fever and could lead to death. A vaccine is available.

CONCLUSION

When living in tropical areas it is advisable to be careful with the intake of raw food, fresh vegetables and water. Avoid ice in drinks and water and do not go for the fresh salad bar even if it looks tempting.

When on business trips, making casual contacts in bars and restaurants with the local guests, try to avoid sexual relationship with these men or women, even if they look appetising, in order to avoid contracting HIV/AIDS. One passionate fling might destroy you and your family's lives.

Since many of the diseases mentioned above are transmitted via blood it is even not advisable to have a shave by a local barber. Pedicure and manicure are also questionable. Bring your own set if you are uncertain of the sterilising equipment.

Do not walk barefoot. In order to avoid being bitten by mosquitos, use mosquito spray and cover your arms and legs in the evenings. When visiting remote areas sleep under a mosquito net.

Finally, do not spoil the enjoyment of your stay in the tropics by becoming paranoid. Use your common sense and learn as you live in your new country.

Chapter Five

THE OUTSIDE WORLD

SAFETY NET

Nationals of traditional Western cultures or from developed countries are generally used to a well organised society with a social system upon which many demands can be made. When we start to live abroad, however, it is important to try to use our own 'wings' when we learn to fly in our new environment.

We are probably not always aware of the fact that we have become dependent on quite strong and reliable social safety nets. We must hold this 'net' for ourselves when making the first moves into the new country.

We are outsiders and quite vulnerable; we cannot make any real demands on the host country, but we can expect services if we can pay for them. Good insurance will ensure that we can pay for whatever we might need in case of theft, sickness, accidents and so forth.

Naturally, there are certain precautions to take and arrangements to make in order for life to run smoothly when establishing oneself in the new country.

EMERGENCIES

The first important weave in a personal safety net is to find out where to go in case of emergency.

A doctor specialising in a certain illness might be needed at night. A good orthopedic surgeon is needed in case you should break a leg. Where is the best and closest hospital? What are the routines? What should you bring when you go there? Must you pay cash before being treated? Where do you find a general practitioner (GP) or a paediatrician? How do you call the police? What do you do in case of fire? What do you do in case of an automobile accident? Simple questions, but try to quickly find the answers.

Make a list of emergency phone numbers – the police, fire department and nearest hospital. Post it on the wall close to the telephone and familiarise the entire family with it.

In general, these and many other questions will be answered by your co-workers or your neighbours, but do find out right away – it is too late when confronted by an acute problem.

SHOPPING

The next step is to find out where to go shopping, where to make the best buys, where to find the specialty stores and so on. Your compatriots will be helpful in giving you advice. Do not hesitate to ask questions. Be curious!

Developing Countries – Getting Started

If you live in a developing country you must find out where the international spouses meet. They can be organised in different ways, but rest assured, they are definitely meeting regularly somewhere and this is your best starting point. They might have published small pamphlets with absolutely wonderful information and sometimes cook books written in the local language. Activities are organised from charity work to bridge and golf. The best thing to do is to attend a meeting and then ask someone to go with you the first time you shop to show you around.

Shopping at various local markets can be interesting and fun, but also time consuming and sometimes frustrating. Bring along your cook if you have one – she will probably be able to help you. Be aware of the fact that prices often rise as soon as salespersons see an expat. Your cook should know how much to pay. Very often, it is best to let her shop there alone.

Bargaining

In many cultures it is important to understand that bargaining is part of any kind of shopping – from vegetables to furniture – and part of the social life. It is not necessarily a way of cheating the customer, but it does not hurt to be on your guard at times. For example, antiques are not always very antique. Bargaining is something you will learn as your stay continues. It may feel very strange and uncomfortable at first if you are not used to this system and it can take a long time before you have come to an agreement. In the meantime, you must be patient and relaxed and keep a smile on your face, even if you are actually swearing under your breath.

FINDING INFORMATION

In order to feel at home quickly and understand the culture and the people in your host country, you must gather information that could be useful. Using the "Cultural Checklist" in Chapter One is one way you will better learn and understand your new country and its nationals. The following topics are also worth looking into to help you gain an insight into exactly where it is you are.

History

An understanding of the history of the people, its wars and important political events, will open new perspectives and facilitate your work and life in the country. It is valuable to recognise the country's famous men and women. If you now live on another continent other than your own, it is interesting – and sometimes frustrating and sad – to find out in what way your new home is connected with your own history.

Geography

Locate your new country on the globe and study its continent. Look at the surrounding countries and familiarise yourself with the country in which you will be living. Narrow it down later to a detailed study of the city in which you live. Buy good informative maps and sample brochures. Some points to consider are:

- What is the population?
- Are there any special facts that you should know?
- Are there areas (both in the country and the city) you should avoid?
- What are the natural resources and what is the country's primary industry?
- What kind of climate can you expect?
- Are there any potential natural disasters, such as volcanoes, typhoons, earthquakes? What precautions should be taken if this is the case?

Political Life

What is the political history and current situation of this country? Who are the most important official persons? Learn what is going on around you. Is the mass media censored? Read the newspapers, both local and international, and compare the articles. What do papers write about? What is the big news? Try to follow the news on TV, install a cable if it is available so that you can watch the international channels or try to find English-speaking programs on the shortwave radio.

YOUR CULTURAL VALUES

Try to keep your own cultural values under control and understand what they really are. It is important to remember that you live in a new culture with a different outlook on the world and on life. Every culture is unique and its members are ethnocentric in that they believe in their own superiority. Thus, we value more our own culture than another culture. Try not to make quick and harsh judgments based on your own 'value pack,' but be objective and observant while listening and learning. Opinions should be formed slowly as you continue to understand a new country and its people. (This initial confrontation with a new culture will sooner or later lead to Culture Shock.)

SECURITY

Security has many meanings. To many, it stands for our whole political system, in which we have been formed and brought up. Safety, security and quality are fundamental concepts in the minds of many nationals of different cultures – values that are reflected in the way we live, think and act.

Our present-day societies suffer from an increase in criminal offences such as robberies, thefts and other violent acts, many of which are drug related. Few countries have been spared from this, although some countries have not yet reached a situation similar to that of the US, for example.

Depending on the country you live in, there are certain 'Dos and Don'ts' you must learn. Pay attention to what people tell you, but do not believe all the horror stories that might be told. It is good to listen and decide for yourself the precautions you want to take. Keep your common sense and be neither overcautious nor negligent.

Missing Children

It is definitely advisable to be on your guard with regards to children, no matter which country you move to, but there are a greater number of potential dangers in countries and cities with large populations.

Accompanying children should be told to be cautious when approached by strangers. Rules must be given and followed. They must learn to phone home and keep you informed about their whereabouts – including teenagers – even if it feels to them as though their freedom is restricted. It is not advisable to hitchhike or accept a ride home from an unknown person.

All children should carry with them a personal ID card with their address and telephone number.

Personal Safety

In a foreign country, you tend to guard your children more than at home, and you always keep a watchful eye when you leave home. You seem to acquire a 'built-in' radar warning system.

There might be a greater risk of being robbed or mugged when living abroad. This is due to many factors. Apart from what is said above, it also has to do with the fact that you often do not look like the nationals living in the country, and you do not speak the language. Avoid carrying around a lot of cash, and keep it in different places in your purse or pockets. To avoid being conspicuous it is not advisable to wear expensive jewels and watches when moving around in large crowds in busy city centres.

Try not to look too frightened and watchful when walking on busy streets among many people; try to feel and look relaxed and melt into the crowd.

A good piece of advice if you are robbed: do not try to get it back. You will easily get a new watch or a purse, but you will certainly not get a new life. Many tragic things have happened in an attempt to recover a stolen item. Stay calm at all times and avoid unnecessary confrontation.

Contact the police and report what has been stolen right away. This is important as your insurance company will require a written police report.

DRIVING

If it is necessary for you to use a car, a driver's licence must be obtained immediately upon arrival. Public transportation is fine in some countries but is not very reliable in others. Much time may be spent in a car, for the working spouse going back and forth to work, and for the accompanying spouse for daily errands – not the least of which is driving children to activities.

It is important to become acquainted quickly with the new area. The traffic flow in most large cities is intense, tiresome and time consuming. Distances, the pace of driving and new traffic rules can create a stressful situation at first. Gradually, you will adjust to the new driving conditions. Bear in mind always to 'look out for the other guy' – driving habits in some countries may be very different to what you are used to. Keep your safety belts on and maintain the good driving discipline that is practised in most countries. And if driving a motorbike, use you safety helmet.

Traffic in a Developing Country – Survival of the Fittest

Most people experience moving around in a developing, overpopulated country as a kind of nightmare. You might as well forget everything you have been taught about safety, courtesy and right of way. Even if there is a rule about right or left hand traffic – it is in general an interesting interpretation of that rule. The traffic is usually congested, the air polluted, the streets often without signs and in poor condition. Many of the cars and vehicles in use would be declared dangerous in many countries.

Some expatriates have a private driver, as it is not recommended for safety reasons to drive alone in certain countries and some local knowledge can be a great time saver. Your driver will become very important to you, and he will be a great help as he will relieve some tension from you in trying to cope with an unusual traffic situation in

57

unfamiliar surroundings. You must not forget to orient yourself in the city, however, in case your driver fails to show up one day.

If an accident happens, make sure a policeman is called right away or, if possible, drive to the closest police station. Do not take unnecessary risks. Be on your guard, be polite and show respect to policemen and other officials. Do not start to negotiate with the persons involved in the accident.

ADJUSTING

You will gradually fit into the social pattern if you have a curious mind and listen to what people tell you. You must also remember that almost all newcomers experience the same feelings and frustrations as yours. Many will be willing to share their feelings and listen to your questions and problems.

A friend once told me a story that she had been told by a missionary working in Africa:

Once, when walking from one village to another with a small tribe, a group of people sat down on the third day and refused to walk any longer. No one understood at first what was wrong; they had plenty of food, much water and had rested at the various stops they had made. After many discussions, it became clear that they had decided to sit down and wait for their souls that had not been able to follow their pace.

Without your soul or 'inner self' you are not a whole human being and cannot function properly. When the souls finally caught up with the tribe, they continued walking with renewed strength.

It is important to remember – even more in this day and age – that travelling so fast between continents may mean that our souls sometimes lag behind. You must be patient when moving to a new country. Sooner or later your soul will catch up with you, too.

After the initial strenuous months, you will feel more at ease and ready to continue to discover your new environment and enjoy your new life.

Chapter Six

CULTURE SHOCK

CULTURE SHOCK
SITI.

When hearing the word 'shock,' you may immediately associate it with the medical term. To be in a state of shock is to experience something terribly frightening or upsetting that has occurred unexpectedly and suddenly. Culture shock does mean that you will go through a state of shock but not, as a general rule, very suddenly. It does not usually imply a serious mental condition, but instead a more long term psychological strain.

FIRST STAGE

The first period in your new environment has been called the 'Tourist Phase.' During this time, you will experience a 'honeymoon' with your newly adopted country (if you have left willingly, that is) and this period could last up to six months, or even longer. This feeling can be compared to a package tour sensation – you concentrate on the similarities between the two cultures and overlook the differences. You in fact enjoy the different lifestyle. It is important to understand that it does not matter in which country you live – the feeling is the same in developing and highly developed countries.

SECOND STAGE

As things settle into a normal routine and you begin to discover your new country, a new phase starts, commonly called the 'Emptiness Phase.' Things that seemed interesting and exotic at first become alien. Values and attitudes are constantly questioned and compared, measured and weighed. Your own values are contrasted with those of the new culture. You feel a loss of norms and experience a mental vacuum. Problems will most likely arise in communication with your co-workers or your newly-found native friends (if you make any!). You might have problems expressing yourself in the new language or even understanding it. Your children will have initial difficulties in their new school situation, missing their old routines, friends and relatives. This will add to a feeling of isolation and misunderstanding. You will miss your own country, the familiar faces, the language and your daily routines, such as reading local newspapers, watching local news and other programs, even those that you might have criticised earlier!

Your new country becomes your enemy; it has deprived you of your basic security, origin and culture. You start to turn against your new country and its nationals, sometimes declaring fairly openly their inferiority to our own culture, making them the scapegoat for the frustration you feel. Naturally, you will glorify your own country in this process of alienation and begin longing for home. This can cause intense discomfort, bitterness, irritability and even depression. Some-times it can also cause actual symptoms of illness.

During this time you will search for comfort in the colony of your countrymen, who often share and recognise many of your reactions. They will be your 'home base' for a certain period of time. Some people tend to remain in this 'colony syndrome' until they move back, never allowing themselves to be assimilated into the new culture.

THIRD STAGE

Slowly, an adjustment will take place, also called the 'Conformist Phase,' which means that you conform and understand the new culture, its ideals and values. This will happen much more quickly if you try to study your country more carefully and learn the reasons why people act the way they do. With a good comprehension of the educational and political system and the upbringing of each individual you will come to an insight of the causes of the differences between your own culture and the new one.

The crisis is over when you feel that you can see, understand and tolerate cultural differences. At this point you have reached an important awareness.

Your sense of humour (we hope you have a good portion) will help you to survive this period, and help you view the problems from a distance. It will even make you joke about your situation and your difficulties.

FOURTH STAGE

You have reached full recovery, also called the 'Assimilation Phase,' when you are able to agree that your foreign culture is just as acceptable as your own – it is just another way of living. You have then assimilated; the new values seem normal and the emotional conflicts and culture clashes begin to diminish.

Naturally, you will grow and mature mentally during this process as you come to an insight about a new culture and a new way of living. You will also be able to see your native culture in a new light, which will lead to a better understanding and improve your self-esteem.

Upon your final return home, you will always cherish the memories you have and dearly miss the country and the people you have left behind. They will stay with you forever.

ADVERSE EXPERIENCE

The 'Emptiness Phase' sometimes develops differently, making you identify totally with your adopted country and turning you away from your national identity. You will 'go native' in order to feel 'in place' in the belief that you will become more accepted. For example, become a cowboy in Texas or adopt a complete Japanese lifestyle. These are often signs of personal insecurity. It is important to hold on to one's basic self; you must not lose your national identity, as your host nationals might feel very uncomfortable dealing with a dual personality.

It is not uncommon to find that persons with this attitude also are highly critical of their own country – something which will further surprise and confuse a host national.

This behaviour might be more common among political refugees as it is important for them to adapt quickly to their new country. However, cultural values buried deep inside will in time pop up again, no matter how hard you try to keep them down.

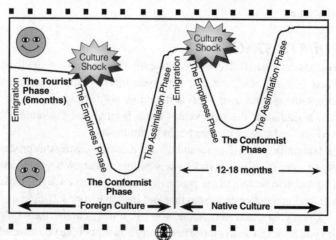

Key Consultants Inc. / M. Rabe

ACCOMPANYING CHILDREN

Your children will very often encounter problems in trying to fit into their new social patterns. They must be accepted by their friends and begin speaking their new language fairly quickly. They feel different and as though they are on the outside; their body language might not be the same as that of their peers, and they often look and dress differently. They have a strong urge to identify quickly with their new culture, as they have not yet grown and matured into independent personalities.

Children sometimes do not feel pride in their national origin and might begin to feel ashamed of their parents and their homes because they are so different to their new surroundings. There is also a language barrier, as most parents have an accent and some speak the new language fairly poorly.

National Pride

You must keep your national pride, however; cherish your cultural background and accept that you are different – which does not mean that you are inferior. You have reason to be proud of your native country and language.

It is often the people in the foreign country who are to blame for their ignorance and prejudice when you do not feel 'at home.'

Many Themes

There are many variations on this theme, and Culture Shock can often be experienced in a modified way. Most likely, however, it is something everybody, child or adult, will go through, independent of their former international experience. It is important to remember that a person faces a totally different situation when actually living in a country. It can never be compared to tourist or business visits, staying at hotels.

No Immunity

Finally, it should be mentioned that you will almost certainly experience culture shock again if you move from one country to another. You are not immune, in other words, if you already have experienced it! Each culture is different and one cannot avoid the process of accepting, rejecting, evaluating and, hopefully, re-accepting an adopted culture.

Some will encounter a more violent culture shock when returning home, as the feeling of alienation then will be in the home country. (See Chapter 17 – Relocation and Repatriation.)

STRESS

Working in a foreign environment, very often within a new business culture, will naturally cause initial stress. We have to learn the new rules of the game and this takes some time. In the beginning your colleagues generally show patience and interest in you but the demands become increasingly higher as times go by. If you encounter unexpected difficulties at work during your culture shock period you will naturally feel tension and stress.

You might, for example, be expected to take initiative, risks and make decisions in a very alien workplace – expectations and opportunities that you have not had at home. You might lack experience and cannot yet read your counterparts and this can result in a great deal of stress.

In order to avoid a 'stressed out' feeling, take a break from routines at times, exercise regularly, read a good book, talk your problems out and stay away from alcohol which only will increase stress and not at all diminish it.

Chapter Seven

LANGUAGE BARRIERS

Native English-speakers are in a fortunate position, as English today is the first means of communication, in a business context, in countries all over the world. Even in the remotest areas you can usually find people who understand and speak English to some degree. It is almost always taught in schools as a second language where English is not the first language and there is an eagerness among young people to learn the language quickly so that they will be able to travel and work abroad. A common language allows us to develop a better understanding of our different cultures and leads to a tolerance and acceptance of differences. In working towards a world without barriers, communication in English is one important tool.

English

As said in the introduction of this book it is essential for speakers of other languages to have a good command of English if chosen for employment abroad. You must be able to communicate with your co-workers and superiors. You should be able to express yourself fairly fluently in both speech and writing.

A Second (or Third) Language

If you are transferred to a country where another language is spoken, it is important that you learn the basics and that you continue to further your education there. It is considered polite in certain countries to be able to greet people and make light conversation in the native language.

The Accompanying Spouse

It is equally important for the accompanying spouse to be able to speak English and, for that matter, any other language that will be needed. It is the spouse who must take care of much of the ground-work, so to speak. Running a house involves many contacts with the outside world, and if children are brought along, the spouse will be needed for making contacts with the school, counsellors and teachers. The children will also need assistance with schoolwork and other assignments.

In certain countries in which most of the population does not speak English, it is of course necessary to quickly learn phrases in the native language that might be helpful when calling for help.

Social Contacts

It is an advantage if you are able to communicate in a local language. Remember that learning a language is challenging, fun and extremely rewarding. Throw away all your inhibitions and start talking – and you will find that many doors will open for you. People are generally very impressed by anyone from another country who can speak their language and often apologise for their own ignorance of foreign languages.

Slang and Other Expressions

When you begin to speak a new language, try to find out if there are certain expressions that you should avoid. Perhaps there are words that should be pronounced differently. There are always words with double meanings; you will learn quickly if you listen carefully and ask questions.

Watch out for 'bad expressions' as you learn the language. It seems sometimes to be easier to swear in a foreign language because the words do not carry the emotional charge that swear words do in your native language. However, they might offend the persons to whom you are talking.

Try to listen to the radio and watch television programs. Listen to what the actors and reporters say. Try to pick up the various idioms, and imitate them by saying the phrases aloud to yourself.

If you are studying another language with a textbook or in a classroom setting, be sure that you combine the book knowledge with the common, standard forms of expression and communication. For example, a textbook or dictionary may teach you to use words or expressions such as "Please extinguish the light," "Good Morning! How do you do?" or "I haven't any beverage yet." However, native speakers, in an everyday use of the language, will speak less formally – "Please switch off the light," "Hi! How are you?" or "I don't have a drink yet." Keep your ears open!

Your children will be your best teachers, as they generally learn the native language or the language at school very quickly. They will correct your pronunciation and teach you the proper phrases and expressions to use. They will eventually lead you through the jungle of slang and other expressions that are in fashion.

Make an effort to read books, newspapers and magazines in the language that you will use most. In this way you will strengthen and accelerate the learning process.

Do You Speak British English or American English?

Depending on the country you are living in you may even have to relearn some key elements of the English language. Many Europeans learn Standard British English at school and find to their great surprise that certain words and phrases just do not work in the United States and many other countries where American English dominates.

Some words are listed below to give you an idea of the differences between British and American English.

British English	*American English*
autumn	fall
banknote	bill
caravan	trailer
cinema	movies
credit account	charge account
dinner jacket	tuxedo
express delivery	special delivery
filling station	gas station
flat	apartment
ground floor	first floor
holiday	vacation
jam	jelly
kerb	curb
lift	elevator
motorway	freeway
number plate	licence plate
pavement	sidewalk

petrol	gas
pram	baby carriage
queue up	line up
railway	railroad
sweet	dessert
tin	can
tube	subway
windscreen	windshield

Chapter Eight

COMMUNICATION

The following story emphasises the difficulties in cross-cultural communication:

The school day ended. Tired Miss Larson took her classroom problems home with her and shared her concerns with friends at an informal cocktail party. She shared her frustration over teaching English in the Ethiopian government school: "For three years, I've tried to get those dear little girls to behave like normal human beings, to have some pride, to hold up their heads, look me in the face, and answer a question in a voice I can hear without straining. They're so bright; they learn as fast as the children back home, but they are hopeless, absolutely hopeless. They just can't seem to learn to behave with human dignity. For all the good I've done here, I might as well have stayed home in Iowa and continued to teach there".

The school day ended. Kebedetch walked stiffly home. The strange steel she had forced into her neck muscles seemed to have spread through her body. She felt rigid, brave but frightened. Entering the *gojo* (small hut), Kebedetch was greeted warmly. Father asked the usual, daily question: "What did you learn today?" Kebedetch threw back her head, looked her father in the eye, and proclaimed in a loud clear voice: "Ethiopia is composed of twelve provinces plus the Federated State of Eritrea." Momma and Poppa talked late that night. What had happened to Kebedetch? She was no longer behaving as a normal human being. "Did you notice how she threw back her head like a man?" asked Poppa. "What has happened to her shyness as a woman?" "And her voice," added Momma.

"How happy I am that our parents were not present to hear a daughter of ours speak with the voice of a foreigner! She showed no modesty; she seemed to feel no pride. If she were normal, she would be ashamed to raise her head like that, being a girl-child, and to speak so loud as that," Poppa added with a deep sigh. "Kebedetch has learned so much," said Momma, "she knows more than I, and this has given me great joy. But if her learnings are making of her a strange, ungentle, beast-like person, I do not want her to learn more; she is my only daughter." Poppa pondered. Finally he shook his head and spoke. "You are right, Mebrat, our daughter must not return to school. The new education is not good, but only the strongest can survive. I had hoped Kebedetch could learn and remain normal and gentle, could become a woman of dignity. The frightening behaviour of her's tonight has convinced me. She has lost her sense of pride, lost her sense of shame, lost her dignity. She must never return to the school. We shall try to help her find herself again!"

—E. Lord in *Examples of Cross Cultural Problems Encountered by Americans Working Overseas: An Instructors Handbook*

COMMUNICATION SKILLS

Communication takes place in the medium of one's culture, which facilitates and reinforces it but also hides it. Communication is buried in our own cultural scene and is difficult to extract and look at.

—Dr. L. Robert Kohls

Culture is, in other words, communication. It is said that although we have communicated throughout the centuries, we still do not quite know why we do not understand each other. The 'miracle' is that despite the fact that we are unaware that we do not know, we are still able to communicate and get along with other people.

Much research has been devoted to communication, and many communication models have been created to explain the various processes that take place when people talk. The basic model most frequently seen is probably the one where we indicate the following:

SENDER ⇒ **MESSAGE** ⇒ **RECEIVER**

The message communicated and how it is received depend on the sender's communication skills, attitude, knowledge and know-how regarding the message. It also has to do with the sender's social status and cultural norms and values. The receiver must possess the same attributes as the sender in order to reach a complete understanding.

CROSS CULTURAL COMMUNICATION

As we often wrongly perceive, misinterpret and misunderstand one another, even when we share many values and attitudes, it is clear that our communication problems will be greater in a foreign country. It is not only that communication is channelled through a foreign language, with words which have different cultural meanings. There is also often a gap between what we want to say and the meanings people attach to our translated message.

We must not take for granted that we all perceive the world in basically the same way, but must be aware of our cultural values. They are often totally different from those of the new culture. It is important to accept this fact and understand that there might be a conflict. There is no real right or wrong – we are all products of our cultural background and upbringing. We must accept the cultural differences, deal with them objectively and see them as assets instead of difficult differences.

The greatest problem in cross-cultural communication is probably that we are not able to listen well. We do not listen to the meaning of the message but only to the words; in other words, we do not listen actively! We must remember to ask questions if we do not understand, because this will spare us from many embarrassing situations later. In return, we must try to be clear and specific, always keeping our cultural values in mind.

Successful cross-cultural communication is the cornerstone of long lasting relationships between you and your host nationals.

BODY LANGUAGE

Communication is not only carried out via a language but also by the use of our 'body language.' Different cultures have different body languages. When we try to give meaning to what we say, we use all kinds of gestures, facial expressions and variations in the tones of our voices. To a person familiar with our culture and language, all this together emphasises the meaning of what we say and reinforces the message. To a person from another culture, our body language could be misinterpreted and even perceived as offensive! We must understand that certain gestures are not accepted in some cultures. It is important to find out what gestures are common in the new culture and to be aware of those that are similar in your own.

DOS AND DON'TS

When arriving in a new country, try to find out right away if there are any 'dos and don'ts' in social life.

Should you shake hands with everyone or only with men? May you look people straight in the eye without offending them? Does a 'yes' mean a 'yes' and is 'maybe' a 'no'? What does it mean to lose face? What will make a person lose face? May you laugh openly? Does a laugh mean that you are just afraid and embarrassed? Are women openly accepted in social situations?

Does waving 'goodbye' mean 'come here' in your new country? What is considered a joke in one culture is not necessarily a joke in another! What makes you angry might not offend a person of another culture.

Is it accepted to burp and pick your teeth openly? May you eat with your fingers or should you use a fork? Is there a hand that is considered 'dirty'?

In Muslim countries, the left hand is 'dirty' and is not used when handing things to another person. (In several other countries in Asia it is regarded polite to hand over things with both hands, however.) It is also common to pinch children's cheeks in some cultures in order to show affection while it is a great offence to touch or pat a child's head to show the same in others, as the head is considered sacred.

Initial Taboos

Do not declare your political views openly or criticise the local political system or leaders. Be diplomatic and show interest in the country. Ask questions and learn as much as possible.

Do not discuss your religious beliefs in a way that might be considered offensive. Religion is very important and fundamental in most cultures and, if you do not have a religious belief, do not openly discuss this initially.

Addressing One Another

If you come from a culture that is considered very informal, both as far as dress code at work and in addressing one another is concerned, you must be prepared to accept that people in many countries adhere to a more formal way of behaving and communicating, using titles and family names rather than first names. The formal use of Mr. and Mrs. is very common all over the world, especially between colleagues and associates, and so it is even in private. There are certain rules when you decide to address each other by first names. Play according to the rules!

You should always use the formal Mr. or Mrs. when talking to your superiors and wait until it is suggested that you use the first name.

When addressing a group of people at an office, for example, you should never use first names in referring to one another.

Your children's teachers will always be addressed by their last names both by you and your children. You as a parent will also be called Mr. or Mrs. by your children's friends, even in an otherwise informal country such as the United States.

First Impressions

As a general rule one could say that it is important to learn about the protocol and etiquette of the country in question, since you should always try to make a good impression. It is important to be polite and attentive as well as being correctly dressed for the occasion.

Remember that you can only make one first impression, so do it right! Appearance, attitude and behaviour are all important parts of communication.

Chapter Nine

SCHOOLS

INTERNATIONAL CHILDREN – OUR GLOBAL NOMADS

Bringing up children abroad in a foreign environment and giving them an international education is usually very rewarding. These children learn to accept changes, challenges and new lifestyles without great effort. They learn to adapt quickly in a new group, make friends easily and become self-reliant. They often also learn one or two new foreign languages and develop a cultural awareness that their compatriot students lack. Their international scope is broad and they become bicultural and generally more open to cultural differences.

However, many children will lose part of their national identity and sometimes develop a rootlessness which may cause problems later on in life – a phenomenon also called 'the global nomad syndrome.' The feeling of home is not as clear to them as it naturally is to youngsters growing up in their native country. They may also be afraid of forming strong relationships as they have found that they seldom last for a long period of time.

Research has been done regarding the psychological and social development of accompanying children. Many ideas are brought forward, but not until recently have we started to focus seriously on these children's personal situations. They have been seen as accompanying baggage and have not been given much attention. Many feel that learning a foreign language has been the foremost experience of growing up abroad. Somehow, we have not fully understood that the foreign language is just a by-product: more importantly, they will learn to adopt a completely new culture through their education in a foreign country. They will be formed and encultured with totally different attitudes, values and norms than those taught in their native schools.

CHANGING SYSTEMS

With this in mind, their entire school situation must be planned and considered before leaving so that they, upon a return to their home country, can easily adjust to the school system with its particular curriculum. They must also be prepared for a difference in values, norms and behaviour.

Boarding Schools

The British and Australian expats, among others, generally seem to leave the upbringing and schooling of their children to boarding schools. They might send their children to these institutions when a child is even younger than 10 years old. The families meet for vacations, and the children grow up independent of their families.

Many researchers have pointed out that it is not advisable to send children to boarding school before the age of 14. Not until then are they emotionally prepared to be separated from their families.

There are of course situations where the only alternative might be a boarding school, for instance for families who are stationed in a country where no education is available. Another reason for choosing a boarding school arises when when the family is likely to be transferred from one country to another. This involves changes of schools, school systems and languages which are unacceptable from a young person's point of view and unwise as far as further education is concerned.

If possible, it is advisable to follow the recommendation of avoiding an early start in boarding schools and bring the whole family on the foreign assignment and thus share the life abroad together.

Diplomats and Businessmen

Although there are many similarities, we must still allow for a difference between the families working within the diplomatic corps and those working for various multinational companies.

Diplomats usually face a whole career abroad, while businessmen normally are only in one country for a period of time and then return home for good. There tend to be cases, however, where you will find business people leading the same life as many diplomats, being transferred from one country to another. This may have to do with their international experience and usefulness but also with a wish on their part to continue to live an international life.

Most corporations recommend families return home after a stay of a maximum of five years in order to avoid becoming rootless. Should you choose a lifelong international career it is important to create a good feeling of home wherever you live. In that way your children will grow up feeling safe and secure. It is of course excellent if you can build up a 'home base' in one country to which you and your family can return regularly.

Alternative Schools

When moving to a foreign country with your children, you must look into what kind of schools are available in the area. As a general rule, you should decide first in what language you wish your children to be educated. In a Western European country there might be a choice between local schools (where the native language is spoken) and English-speaking schools. You will even find in the large cities small native-language (i.e. your first language, if other than English) schools operating.

A native-language school with a good curriculum and competent teachers is an excellent alternative, if available. Your children will have a good education, maintain and develop their native tongue, and learn the language spoken in the country, in addition to English. They will also take all the subjects required by your country's National School Board, and are thus prepared to jump right into their own system without difficulty when moving home again.

The only disadvantage of a small native-language school is, of course, limited resources and, with this, fewer activities. The children can feel somewhat isolated and their international experience could be restricted. There is a risk that they will not make any friends among their host countrymen or any other foreign students.

Local or International Schools

If there is a choice between a local and an international English-speaking school, the latter is definitely to be preferred. English is the dominant international language and in case of a transfer to another country, you will most likely find an English/American International school there. It will in other words facilitate your transfer tremendously.

North America – Public or Private Schools

When moving to North America, you might consider enrolling your children in a private school. As said earlier, private schools are costly, and most companies do not make extra allowances for private schools. These schools are usually smaller and more familiar, with fewer students in each class. More attention and care is spent on each student. As they are private enterprises, they must maintain a good academic standard to maintain a sufficient number of students.

Public schools are commonly very large with fairly big classes and, to students who may be used to smaller schools, they may at first seem frightening. However, the best schools (with dedicated teachers) will be found in good neighbourhoods, and one must not forget that there is competition between the various local schools not only in sports but also in academic achievement. The school's reputation is always in focus and at stake.

Schools in the United States

American schools face many problems today, as they have limited budgets and in certain areas a great influx of immigrants from many parts of the world. Some schools also have racial problems. Recruitment of teachers can pose a problem in certain states because of low salaries, poor working conditions and social difficulties. The quality of education naturally varies from state to state and must be considered separately.

You can obtain all the necessary information regarding the schools in your area from the local School Board. You can check the ranking of the school and its placement in nationwide academic tests. These show the students' average test scores and the percentage of students enrolling in college or university education.

INTERNATIONAL SCHOOLS

Private, independent international schools are usually American-sponsored, and they are likely to be found in the major cities of the world, primarily because of a fairly large American expatriate colony.

The curriculum of the international schools reflects the international attendance and is not strictly American oriented. The faculty is international, with high academic qualifications, and the schools are usually large, modern and have many facilities. Classes are normally kept small.

Graduation requirements follow American recommendations. Textbooks and all other material is American. Many schools offer I.B. (International Baccalaureate) courses. Education in international schools is generally excellent.

ESL – English as a Second Language

When you as a foreigner enroll your children in an American or international school, the children will be tested in English and mathematics. If they have no previous experience in English, they will be placed in a special program where they will be taught English intensively.

They will most likely have one or two ESL classes per day at first, but will generally learn very quickly and be placed in the ordinary classes usually after the first semester.

The American School System

The American school system ranges from K (Kindergarten) to grade 12. It is divided into three parts: Lower School (K-6), Middle School or Junior High School (7-8), and Upper School or High School (9-12).

The School Year

The school year can be divided into two or three semesters, starting in August and ending in June. There are usually three major breaks in the year: Christmas, spring and Easter.

Grades

The two-semester year is split up into four quarters, with a marked grade period after each quarter. In some schools, final exams are given in each individual subject once a year and in others after each semester. These are based on what the students have studied throughout the semester. The students must pass all the exams and other requirements; if they do not, they will be held back one year.

The following grades are generally given:

A (Superior)   **D** (Below Average)

B (Above Average)   **F** (Failing)

C (Average)

Grade Scale: (local school board in Virginia, USA)

A – 94–100%   **D** – 70–77%

B – 86–93%   **F** – below 70%

C – 78–85%

Most schools use an A to F grading scale and a 0 to 100% numerical scale, but the percentage equivalents may vary slightly from this chart. Check with the school concerning their system.

There is usually further testing during the school year (in all grades), including local, state and nationwide tests.

Students in grades 11 and 12 are tested regularly by a so-called SAT test (Student Aptitude Test) in order to qualify for college.

During the quarters, the students are given Progress Reports or Report Cards that inform you about your child's progress. You will always be informed if you need to help your children with their schoolwork.

Discipline

School discipline in the international schools is fairly strict in comparison to the Scandinavian school systems, for example, though this varies somewhat between schools. There are punishments or restrictions if rules and regulations are not followed. Talking in class is not accepted. The teachers have authority and demand the respect of their students.

Students can be given 'detention' if they repeatedly disobey rules, meaning that they will have to stay after school or during their study time and work under supervision.

If they continue to be difficult, they will be 'suspended' from school for a certain amount of time, depending on the offence. The worst punishment is being 'expelled,' – not allowed to stay in the school.

Lower School

Subjects taken in Lower School concentrate on reading, writing and mathematics, as in most schools in the world. Other subjects are: social studies, P.E. (Physical Education), art and music. There is much creativity incorporated in the learning methods. Report cards are given starting in grade K. Much emphasis is placed on competition, awards and merits. Diplomas are handed out regularly to students who achieve or improve the most. There are special programs for gifted children as well as for those who have learning difficulties.

The teachers change for each grade the children attend. Sometimes a teacher can have his class in two consecutive grades, but this is very rare. The classes are also very often broken up, and classmates are not necessarily the same as the previous year.

The general school philosophy is to foster independent human beings ready to accept that they live in an ever-changing world where everyone must rely on his own capabilities.

Middle School

Middle School starts preparing the students for High School. Here they will have one teacher for one subject, and will start more independent studies. The transition from the Lower School to Middle School could be dramatic and full of tension, but much help is available and it usually goes very smoothly.

Subjects taken are: English, math, science, history, geography, French, German or another foreign language, P.E., art, music, drama and some other elective subjects.

Upper School

Upper School or High School is the final stage in education and is aimed toward preparing students for college and university studies. There are, however, many options for vocational training and classes that are oriented towards more practical occupations.

Credits

In order to graduate from High School, students must have earned approximately 22 CREDITS (varying from state to state, but usually about 22 to 24). They earn one credit per subject during one full school year, but it is sometimes also possible to take one-semester courses and receive half a credit per semester. They must pass each class to get one credit. There are certain basic requirements in terms of subjects in granting diplomas.

OUR NATIVE TONGUE

It is essential to stress the importance of keeping the native language active within your family while living abroad. Depending on the time spent abroad, this need may vary, but in the case of a stay in a foreign-speaking country longer than one year, the accompanying children must have some continuous education in their native language.

ONE PERSON – ONE LANGUAGE

Research in this area strongly recommends that the native language is spoken in the home. Do not encourage a second language in the home if you as parents share the same language. In case each parent has their own language, the rule 'one person, one language' should be obeyed from the beginning of a child's first communication until at least the age of three years. The child will then become bilingual. There might be cases when a third language is spoken in the family between the parents, and in this particular case the child might become trilingual, but it is recommended to stress the two languages at first.

There are various ideas regarding the upbringing of a child in several languages. It is usually best to give the child a solid foundation as far as the native language is concerned. A child is supposedly ready for a second language at the age of ten to twelve years.

The native language is an emotional language through which the parents have given the child love, affection and security. It is part of a person's roots and cultural heritage. With two languages, you receive two identities. If a language is not nurtured and encouraged, it will fall behind and stop in its development. A bilingual child must use both languages actively to avoid the risk of using one to convey sentiments and the other – often the language used at school – as the academic language.

A Language Dilemma

It is true that it is extremely rewarding to be able to manage two languages equally well. Our children will no doubt be able to express themselves fluently, often without an accent, after a couple of years' exposure to a foreign language. We must be aware of the fact, though, that they will seldom acquire the vocabulary that their national fellow students have, and that there is a great difference in the knowledge of the language that our children have as compared with their class-mates, for the simple reason that it is their native language. Conse-quently, they run the risk of acquiring a limited vocabulary in both languages. In the long run, they will concentrate on their new language and benefit from this academically, but this will be at the cost of their native tongue.

Pride and Prejudice

Many parents take pride in the fact that their children somehow are different and can master a foreign language. This is fully understand-able, but it is not an excuse for ignoring the native language. Many problems with repatriation will be avoided if the children continue to speak their first language fluently.

It is not going to be helpful to them to be linguistically handicapped when trying to readjust to their home country. They will have enough cultural obstacles to tackle since they do not have the same frame of references as their schoolmates who have remained in their own country. Your children will have a lot of catching-up to do – both academically and socially when once returning home. Remember that they have had 'time-out' from their own culture and they need all your help to re-adapt.

85

Chapter Ten

SINGLE LIFE

In most countries of the world, the male and female roles are clearly defined. Men are traditionally the breadwinners and heads of the families, while women stay at home with their children. Patriarchal societies are most common. Equality between women and men – both in a professional and social sense – still has a long way to go.

INDEPENDENT WOMEN

We are seeing all over the world a gradual change of attitudes among the younger generations. Women are better educated today and can and will make demands on society. They are a strong and underestimated work force, who in the future will change our views of work by introducing a more feminine approach in our business cultures. This means that we will have to respect and accept that women also must be able to combine a family life with a professional career. So far women are the only ones who are able to give birth to babies!

In the Scandinavian countries, for example, a majority of all women are gainfully employed and most are economically independent. Men and women are co-workers in these societies, sharing not only economic responsibilities but also household duties and child care. Generous allowances and maternity leaves are granted to all mothers in connection with a child's birth. Men are encouraged to share the maternity leave and care for the baby. This might be considered very strange in other cultures. The concept of a 'unisex' has come far in these countries. However, we must bear in mind that this is not the case everywhere and we will not find the same attitudes in most developing countries, for example, where 'Daddy knows best!'

MALE DOMINATION

We are well aware of the fact that the male dominates within the business world. It is therefore usually not difficult for a single man to become established abroad. This refers to business, social and cultural situations. A man is readily accepted wherever he goes. His 'cards' have already been given and his only problem is to play them according to the rules of the culture in which he lives. (Women, however, experience a much tougher play.)

Single Males

Being single and male offers many social challenges. In most cultures, a man can move about freely and visit restaurants, bars and other establishments without being looked down upon. There do not seem to be any barriers or dangers that would stop a man in his new culture. In many cultures it is only a man's world, and the married and single women must remain in their homes.

Dating

Dating a woman in a Western culture usually follows the same pattern where ethic and moral values may vary a bit but are not difficult to decode.

87

Dating a woman in a non-Western culture may be more troublesome, however, and should also be done with more consideration and care. We must take into account all the values that play a part in the various cultures. Women in these cultures might not be as 'sexually available' (the 'professionals' are not taken into account here), and a certain type and time of courtship might be expected. Be aware of the fact that what you consider a casual date can, in certain countries, be understood as the beginning of a relationship leading to marriage.

It is extremely important to remember that we have great cultural differences, and that we are guests in a foreign country and must try to play according to the rules. You as an expatriate will one day leave, but your friends and the memory of you will remain. Be careful to avoid hurting other human beings by not being serious or honest.

On the other hand, you can also be a target for some who see your position and above average earnings as an easy mark. Relationships should proceed with some degree of caution – make sure both partners are aware of what the other intends before committing too much too quickly.

Loneliness

Being single does not necessarily mean that life is full of action and fun after working hours. There will be times when you feel lonely and isolated. In particular if you live in a developing country you might become frustrated with the lack of entertainment, such as convenient movies and theatres, libraries, art museums, sporting facilities or problem-free weekend travels. Spending every night in bars and restaurants becomes boring. People come and go and you have to make new friends over and over again. The result could be that you spend too much money on alcohol which in the long run could be a disaster.

There is no one there to share with you the frustrations and personal emotions that you might experience. It is essential that you have a strong character and an ability to reach out and find lasting friends and support.

Reading books and studying the foreign language and culture will make you feel more settled. Sports activities such as tennis, squash or golf are excellent therapies against boredom and isolation.

Marriages and Dangerous Liaisons

Single men very often return home as married men, bringing both wife and children. This is probably an indication that the basic need for a family and personal security often overrules the hectic bachelor's life!

It must be remembered that single, professional men are much 'in demand' in certain countries, in particular countries with closed borders and restrictions for the nationals to leave their country. A marriage to an expat could mean an 'escape' into a new freedom or a life that seems adventurous and luxurious. Beware that life in a suburb in your home country is not the same as living in an expat colony far away from home. Approach new relationships with a realistic attitude, discuss your cultural differences and be prepared for a difficult readjustment period on your return home. A bicultural marriage means that you must accept living with two sets of core values and norms, and tolerate and respect one another within that framework.

89

SINGLE AND PROFESSIONAL WOMEN

Single professional women may not have the same easy going time as their male colleagues. Married professional women undergo a similarly difficult situation; they, in addition, must face the social pressure of bringing a male spouse to their host country which is definitely not yet socially accepted in most cultures.

If a professional woman must work very hard in order to become accepted as an equal in a male-dominated Western business world, she will have an even tougher time in most non-Western cultures.

In many other societies, a woman is not regarded as an equal. She is supposed to be married, have children and serve her family in every respect. She is expected to help and support her husband in his career.

It involves much hardship to become accepted as a professional woman, to be taken seriously and have people listen to you. Often the emphasis is more on the way you look and how you dress than what you know and what you say. Women who talk about self-fulfilment and have a strong desire to stress their personal identity are unfortunately still regarded with suspicion in many cultures. However, professions within the medical and educational field are more readily accepted than those within business and technology, for example.

In order to cope, you need the following assets: patience, toughness, self-confidence, self-control and determination. There are a small number of women working internationally and they deserve all our admiration and respect.

Dating

To date a man from a non-Western culture is difficult, as marriage always seems to be the motive for dating. In Western cultures, the rules of the game are easier to learn and understand as long as you are aware of the fact that women from countries considered 'sexually liberated' could be expected to start casual affairs on the spur of the moment. It is good advice not to live up to that image!

Lonely Life

Life as a single woman can become difficult and isolated at times, much like that of single men. The bar scene is not really the choice of a single professional woman, particularly in developing countries.

However, it is important to reach out quickly and activate oneself. Work alone will not be sufficient. Again, it is advisable to join a sports or social club, take up a new interest or hobby and get involved in society. There is much to learn. New friends will be made – often they will be people who are in the same situation as yourself. Usually you will find friends very quickly among your colleagues or compatriots and they will form a support group that you will need from time to time as a single person abroad.

DANGEROUS LOVE LIFE

In many countries the threat of sexually transmitted diseases may be more prevalent than it is in your own country. The deadly disease, AIDS (Acquired Immune Deficiency Syndrome), has been named the new plague of this century. It is well worth considering the seriousness of this statement.

As we all know, AIDS is a common disease among men, women and children in Africa and has spread via the Caribbean into America, Europe and Asia afflicting homosexuals as well as heterosexuals, intravenous drug users and haemophiliacs. AIDS is, however, spreading rapidly in the developing countries due to a lack of knowledge of the disease among the general populations, and how to avoid contact with the virus.

Prostitutes

A large number of prostitutes in these countries (male and female) are infected with HIV (Human Immunodeficiency Virus; eventually leading to AIDS) and since it is transmitted sexually you should take all precautions and be on your guard. Your life and many other persons' lives may be at risk. Consult with your physician and take his advice seriously.

Most other venereal diseases are curable if detected at an early stage, and if you suspect that you have contracted an ailment of this order – see a doctor right away.

Chapter Eleven

STAYING TOGETHER

When a family is transplanted into a new culture it will go through much hardship in adjusting to the new country. As mentioned earlier, culture shock is part of the adjustment to a new and foreign lifestyle. A positive attitude and a readiness for the challenges ahead will facilitate life tremendously.

GREAT EXPECTATIONS

All family members will not only feel much pressure, but also a great deal of expectation, during the initial period abroad. In order to reach a positive outcome from this mixture of strange emotions, everyone must chip in and do his share to make things work. There must be an openness to signs of tension created by culture shock or other causes.

You must be patient and help each other through difficult times. Try to keep communication open within the family, talk about your reactions and emotions and be aware of new signs of different behaviour in each other's characters. Show each other trust, love and forgiveness. If you manage to weather this severe test, your family will come out much stronger than it was before you left. You will find that bonds have been created between family members that are difficult to break.

DIVORCES

Unfortunately, many families cannot endure all the hardship that is placed on them, and in many instances families break up for good. It can be argued whether they would have failed anyway, but as this is a hypothetical question it will remain unanswered. The fact remains however that you can never flee from problems and if you brought some with you they will most likely grow larger in an alien environment.

As long as everyone understands the 'importance of being earnest,' family ties will become stronger and the unity unbreakable.

THE WORKING SPOUSE

The person who has been assigned this new position is greatly pressured in terms of performance. Many new situations will be faced and many tricky problems solved before communication between all parties begins to function properly. It always takes time to feel comfortable in a new job. It is usually necessary to spend much more time away from home. The working hours are sometimes unbearable, and there are certain demands on you socially that you might not have faced before. Your work becomes more important than your home, and there are many conflicts between your loyalty to your company and your family.

All this is still generally very rewarding, both economically and personally, and an assignment abroad is always regarded as a challenging time in your career when you have the opportunity to learn, develop and share your knowledge with others in a foreign environment. You will naturally feel extremely frustrated at times, when you cannot decode the messages given to you. A successful assignment will make you grow personally and give you a new outlook on your company and even on your life.

Your Family and Their Needs

It is important, however, to keep in mind that the rest of your family needs you too, and sometimes more time than you are able to give. Consider the following points regarding your life at home:

- Try to spend as much time as possible with your family.
- Keep them informed about your whereabouts and your work.
- Share your experiences with your spouse, as she is usually not working and might be thirsting for contacts with the outer world.
- Try to discover your new country together whenever there is a chance.
- Make contacts and have an active social life.
- Take up a new hobby or sport in which you all can take part.
- Stay faithful and loyal to your spouse and family.

THE HOMEMAKER

The person who stays at home and takes care of the house and family is nowadays called 'homemaker.' And this is what you do – you try to make your home as livable as possible and you are usually in full charge of the whole home business.

Depending on the country you will move to, you will play different roles as a homemaker but, whatever your role, it is extremely important to make your home friendly and open. If you fail as a 'homemaking spouse,' the rest of the family's existence is on very shaky ground. This could lead to great problems for everyone. Again, approach your vital task with a positive attitude.

JOBLESS

Many working women are used to a hectic working day, both at home and at work. Not many accompanying spouses have the privilege to continue their professional careers while living abroad. In many countries, it is virtually impossible to obtain a work permit for an accompanying spouse. This could be a difficult situation to face, if her job has become vital to her wellbeing as well as her independence. To many women an interesting job and colleagues play a very important role, and so does the salary.

LOST INDEPENDENCE

If you are used to being economically independent, it is difficult at first to accept that you are only on your spouse's payroll. You will feel that you have lost your independence and own value, because you are used to handling your own economy. You will naturally miss your job and friends at work. Your only source of communication with the outside world at first is your spouse, who in turn might have difficulties adjusting to a new job. Your spouse must recognise these feelings and show you generosity and allow you spending money and freedom.

However, we must keep in mind that this is a stage that will pass if you remember to rid yourself of these values for a while. Your personal value does not lie in a professional career only. There are other things in life to discover. Many people enjoy this free time from jobs and other demands. It can be a great luxury to have so much free time at one's disposal, and an excellent opportunity to enjoy small children. To be in charge of a home is a challenging and worthwhile occupation if you approach it positively.

If you have a family, you will note that your day circles around the children and their activities. You will become their driver, as the transportation facilities are not reliable in many large cities. The children will also need your help in doing their homework and you will be asked to assist with many of their after-school activities. They will make new friends – and so will you.

DEVELOPING COUNTRIES

Moving to a developing country, on the other hand, involves a completely new experience. There you may be in charge of a staff of servants that will help you in your domestic work. You will be their supervisor and they will relieve you of many daily chores. You will be fully occupied with this new life situation for a fairly long time but, once used to the system, you will most likely love it.

There will be many problems at first in communicating and you must be prepared to face many strange and comic situations, but be patient and aware of the cultural differences that exist and try to understand why you do not always understand each other. You cannot expect your domestic employees to share your cultural values. They might learn from you and at best, you will learn from them. When giving instructions to servants, be explicit, talk slowly and make them repeat what you have said. Remember that in many Asian cultures, for example, people must never say no in order not to 'lose face.' They will thus always answer yes even if they do not understand. Finally, avoid confrontations and keep your temper!

In many of these countries, you may also have a car and a driver, so he will take a heavy burden from your shoulders in transporting your children from one place to another.

DEPRESSION AND CURES

There is no doubt that you as a homemaker will feel depressed and isolated many times. The only cure for boredom is to reach out and make new contacts. Discover the new community and see what makes it special. This is the time when you should try to concentrate on that new hobby or sport that you have had in mind for a long time. Get involved in a club or association or some volunteer work. Keep yourself busy. Discover local or native foods and experiment with them in your menus. If you have children, get involved in your children's schools-they often need many volunteers.

Perhaps you would like to study – there are excellent courses available in most places. You can take a local language class or some other interesting classes. You can also study more intensively through correspondence courses. If this is the case, do not be disappointed if you do not succeed. It takes much discipline to finish a course by correspondence on one's own. The best alternative in this case is to study together with someone else; that way, you can inspire one another to continue.

ACCOMPANYING CHILDREN

Your children will also experience a culture shock in some way or other, not always as significant as yours. They will sooner or later realise that they are not on a vacation and that the stay in the new country will last for a seemingly very long time. They will miss their friends and relatives.

They might feel insecure and left out in the new school environment and they need time to adjust. There must however be a limit to how much you should give of yourself as a parent. The children (if they are old enough) must be made aware of the fact that this assignment is something you have agreed upon and all must make an effort to make it work.

Small Children

Small children are usually easy to take along as they will be with the family and not really confronted with the world around them. Consider it a privilege to stay home with your small children and follow them as they develop in their early childhood. The first three years of a child's life are very important for his future development. Be there and help them grow.

Teenagers

Teenagers still in search of their personality often experience a move as very dramatic before they feel that they fit into their new social roles. They often feel that their security is threatened. Strong friendships that have been formed in their home country must be broken and new ones formed. Adjustment to a new school, new routines and regulations and sometimes stricter discipline – both at school and in social life – is fairly painstaking. On top of this they might experience much pressure academically, if they are expected to function in a new foreign language. Give them information, help and support.

Dating

In most European countries and North America, teenagers are able to move freely about and associate with friends, both male and female, casually. In many other countries there are strict rules as to dating a girl or meeting a boyfriend. There are many different views on morality, dating and sex. It is true that teenagers in certain Western countries have a completely different outlook on these matters than young people of many other countries. If you come from a culture with a more liberal, straightforward and open-minded approach in these questions, remember that this is a matter of values that must be handled with care. Talk to your teenagers and try to discuss these matters with them. Keep your children informed and encourage sex education at an early age. Arm them with the knowledge to make the right decisions.

On the whole, one might say that a teenager's existence is usually more guarded and sheltered while living abroad. Parents play a much more dominant role in a teenager's life internationally. The accompanying teenager's only retreats might be their school and the activities there.

Alcohol and Drugs

What is of great concern today is the widespread use of alcohol and drugs. It seems as though both are available everywhere, even if they are forbidden by law. As a parent, you should inform your teenagers about the dangers in using drugs and also keep a watchful eye over them. Remember that in certain countries handling or using drugs could be punished by death.

WHAT EVERYBODY SHOULD KNOW ABOUT DRUGS

Marijuana

Marijuana, also called pot, grass, dope or weed is the most well known and commonly used drug among teenagers and adults all over the world.

It consists of greenish-brown dried leaves, small stems and flowering tops of the plant cannabis sativa. There are over 400 different chemicals in marijuana of which THC is the primary mind-altering ingredient. Hashish or hash oil are processed forms of marijuana and contain up to 20% THC, while marijuana usually has a content of around 4%. Marijuana is usually smoked as cigarettes called joints.

The effects of the drug vary from person to person but are similar to being mildly drunk. The noticeable mental effects include a changed sense of time and difficulty in concentrating. The short-term memory is also affected, as is a person's reaction time.

In the early 1970s, people believed that marijuana was a less harmful drug than cigarettes and alcohol, but today research has suggested that this drug is extremely harmful and hazardous. Apart from being harmful to the body, it has serious mental effects. It can cause apathy, and a lack of motivation, concentration and memory.

Heroin

Also called smack, junk, horse or hammer, heroin is an extremely addictive drug. It usually comes in the form of a white powder. It can be injected or sniffed. It affects the nervous system, reduces the ability to feel pain, and causes drowsiness. It is a very dangerous drug and can cause coma or death in cases of overdose.

Cocaine

Cocaine comes from the coca plant which grows in South America and is sold in the form of white powder. As it is very expensive, it is mixed with other substances that look like cocaine.

It is usually 'snorted,' that is, sniffed through the nose, but can also be injected or smoked through a process called 'freebasing.' It has a rapid effect, and the user feels energetic and euphoric.

The appetite is also reduced. The 'high' feeling lasts for a very short time and is followed by a feeling of depression, which leads to a desire for more of the drug to dispel this feeling.

It is a very addictive drug and heavy users risk their lives by taking overdoses which may result in heart and lung failure.

Crack

Crack or rock is a highly potent, addictive form of cocaine. It is usually smoked, but can also be snorted.

It is a fairly new drug, usually coming from South America, and is at present considered cheap, easily available and 'safer' than heroin, which must be injected. The AIDS risk has made many addicts turn to crack instead.

Crack consists of cocaine, baking soda and water, which is heated, dried and broken into tiny pieces and sold as crack rocks. They are usually smoked in glass pipes. It is a very compulsive drug, and its effect is so intense and powerful that it makes the users think of nothing else but the next 'smoke.'

Amphetamines

These generally come in the form of pills and are called speed, uppers and pep pills among others. The effects are exaggerated activity, irritability and nervousness. Some users can stay awake for as long as six days in a row, but the 'crash' that occurs after the drug wears off can be hazardous.

LSD and Mescaline

These two drugs are also dangerous and mind-altering. LSD is commonly called acid and comes in a liquid form, mescaline is called mesc or cactus and comes in the form of slices from the cactus plant peyote.

Ecstacy

Ecstacy is the most common of the so called 'designer drugs.' It is taken in the form of a small pill and gives the user a heightened sense of euphoria and energy. It is most commonly associated with dance clubs and parties. Because it is difficult to detect and easy to take it has become popular among teenagers and young adults.

Adjusting

Young people usually have a much easier time 'swimming in new waters,' as they do not have all the prejudices and values that we as adults have accumulated though the years. They are actually much more ready to face new situations than we dare to believe. They will lead you into a new culture, make you aware of new educational systems and give you an insight into new ways of thinking.

In fact, they might be your best guides in learning how to adjust to a new country if you are willing to let go of some of your own long held values.

Chapter Twelve

WORKING LIFE

BUSINESS CULTURES

In order to be able decode a country's business culture you need a deep insight into the local culture. Obviously, this needs some work and an inquisitive mind, but much research is being done worldwide and excellent literature and other publications are available. Universities and other international organisations all over the world offer a wide variety of seminars and lectures in this area.

If you are going to do business or work in a country that is unknown to you, try to prepare yourself carefully before leaving. Even if the country in question feels familiar, keep in mind that there is a great difference between coming on regular business visits and actually staying on a long term basis in the country. Living and working in a foreign country will place much greater demands on you since you are expected to know and follow the local rules which also include values, attitudes and behaviour. These rules cannot be learned without the help of your colleagues, who have lived in the area as expats before you, or your new local colleagues. You might, however, also need local expertise in the form of qualified local consultants.

A good starting point to broadening your knowledge of the culture is to understand the importance of the social structures in the society of which you are going to be a part. In order to make this more understandable we will start looking at two types of societies and then try to fit our own country as well as our new country into one of the two. We will then discover differences and similarities which hopefully will serve as real eye-openers.

Strong States

Many countries have created societies based on a very strong state, which means that the public sector is extremely significant to all the members of the society. Laws and the making of laws are important and the members of this particular society are supposed and expected to live according to what has been decided. The judiciary institutions enforce the laws together with a police force that protects the people in a basically honest way. The governing politicians and leaders are chosen democratically and represent the majority of the people. The ideas and fundamental concepts are introduced with the help of these politicians but also by educators and the mass media.

The lives of the people are in fact in the hands of the state which collects taxes that are distributed equally in the various sectors of the society. In many but not all of these countries people are well cared for even before birth till death through a system of welfare. These social benefits could range from maternity care, child care, equal education, health care, old age care and pension plans to help with funeral costs. Nationals growing up and living in this type of state-run country expect and demand all kinds of benefits and services, from hospitals to roads and transport systems, in return of the various taxes collected from them through a working lifetime.

Weak States

Other countries have not developed into these strong states but could rather be classified as 'weak' states which means that the public sector is weak or non existent. The state as such could even be considered hostile and disruptive and often corrupt. Laws and the implementation of laws are not always respected and obeyed, while the religious laws very often are more important and well regarded. The ruling leaders can come from influential families who have held power for generations but they can also be appointed and sometimes even self-appointed – in other words they have taken power of the country together with a small elite, very often with a military background. We have even seen in certain states that leadership can be inherited by the widow of an assassinated leader. Civil servants and the police force are very often corrupt, taking bribes to complement their incomes.

The public sector is likewise fairly insignificant and the lives of the people are more in the hands of the people and their large families. Birth rate depends on religious or practical reasons such as social security or family pressure. Care for the family members is in the hands of the family. Depending on the social and economic status of the family the members can have a life in extreme wealth or appalling poverty. Education is available in small community schools, private schools, religious schools or expensive international schools depending on background and social status. Health care could be excellent for a few while the majority have to rely on healers or self-help. Foreign aid often plays a dominant part in these countries' structures as they emerge as developing countries.

IDENTIFICATION

Many European countries have strong states with a large social commitment which have become a burden since the collected tax money does not cover all the social obligations. This has created unrest and distrust among the people who feel that the politicians have a hard time living up to what they have promised. In certain states one has been forced to dismantle some of the social benefits. Nevertheless most people still feel that they should continue to support the system that has been created during the last fifty years.

In other countries we recognise traits from the so called weak states. The families play, for example, an extremely important role in social as well as business life. The families depend solely on upon each other, creating strong social knots that often are impossible to untie.

In the United States, for example, we will find an interesting mixture of both systems. In general, people do distrust a strong governing state and 'individual freedom' is highly regarded. Many want to be in charge of their own lives and have a freedom to choose or decide what schools to choose, health care program to opt for etc., while still a minority would like to see more social programs on the political agenda. On the other hand the federal authorities have a great deal to say, in particular when it comes to paying or rather avoiding paying taxes.

It is important to keep in mind that we are all basically brought up in one of these systems which we also generally have accepted. The identification process is important to go through in order to come to a better self understanding and thereby also understand that most cultures have varied solutions.

However, we must also accept that there are no wrong or right ways of doing things – only different ones. We must try to avoid being judgemental.

INTERCULTURAL UNDERSTANDING

As said above there are many excellent international intercultural consultants working within this field and one of the more famous European experts is Geert Hofstede who has introduced an interesting way of looking at the world's business cultures.

He studies and compares our societies from the following five concepts regarding intercultural interactions in the workplace.

Individualism – Collectivism

He compares here the actual organisation of the society and to what degree a group membership determines whether or not the goals are met. He contrasts *Collectivist Societies*, in which it is very important to be a long-term member of a group, with *Individual Societies* where there is a tolerance and sometimes encouragement of workers who choose to work by themselves and even reach individual goals.

Power Distance

Very briefly, this is a judgement of the degree (high or low) that separates one hierarchical level from another in a business culture.

Cultures with *high power distance* have pyramidal organisations with strong hierarchy, controlled and supervised work and limited work field. Communication is carried through 'in rank.' Social status is very important as well as seniority (age), academic titles and achievements.

In cultures with *low power distance* we find flat organisations with less hierarchy. Work is often independent and delegated and the control is less supervisory. Communication is usually flexible and equality is important between women and men. Education, social status and titles are not always emphasised.

Masculinity – Femininity

In general one could say that this is about people's concerns and preferences in the workplace. In *masculine business cultures* we find more men in the workplace, in particular within the leadership, and women are relatively powerless in the decision-making process. There is a strong emphasis on salaries and advancement on the job, strong competition between individuals and ample opportunities and demands to remain up to date.

In *feminine business cultures* we find a strong female representation, even politically, and there is an emphasis on cooperative relations with supervisors and co-workers. On the whole it is important to maintain a friendly work atmosphere which also reflects the work environment. The societies in these cultures are more organised to support working women while starting up a family by granting maternity leaves and creating day-care facilities for the children.

Uncertainty Avoidance

In short this is a measurement of the number of rules and regulations commonly found within a country and its business culture. In countries with *high uncertainty avoidance* we encounter heavy bureaucracy with red tape and strong regulations in order to, for example, avoid risks. It can also involve thorough feasibility studies and other activities before starting up various business projects in order to avoid loss of invested money.

Hight Power Distance Organizations

Formalities (titles, last names)
Dress Code
Infomation "in rank"
Controlled and supervised work
Hierarchy
Social Differences

Low Power Distance Organizations

Less formalities
No dress code
Flexibility in information
Independent work, delegation
Less supervision
Less hierarchy
Strive for equality

Key Consultants Inc. / M. Rabe

Confucian Dynamism

This is an extremely important factor in Asian countries and it involves the relative influence (high, moderate or low) of the philosophical principles formulated by Confucius. Above all it deals with the importance of relationships within a business culture where strong family units are important. Hard work and perseverance are other values that are essential, based on mutual obligations and avoidance of losing face. The importance of family relations in business transactions are equally important in Latin American countries.

CULTURE CLASHES

Having all the above in mind we fully understand that a person, representing one culture completely different from the culture in which he or she is going to work, will encounter various culture clashes. It involves simple things like body language, small talk, display of emotions, gestures, dress code, formalities and greetings – in other words appropriate behaviour. We must try to understand a culture's taboos or dos and don'ts in order to avoid the most common cultural mistakes and behave in a manner that demonstrates knowledge and respect for the way of conducting business in the actual culture in which we are going to function.

Male and Female Roles

We must also become aware of the fact that women are treated differently in various cultures, ranging from total equals and co-workers to subordinates without any or little input. The fact remains that it is important to be flexible and open to new situations. The way to succeed is to understand the underlying cultural values that have formed the basis of the business culture in question.

Truly international persons must have the ability to work as equals with people of diverse background – both men and women.

Intercultural Teaching

Many expatriates working within international education truly face a great challenge and experience a different dynamism when working with international students and teachers. Having the cultural discussion in mind we understand that it requires much flexibility when trying to make students from very different cultures cooperate and develop individually while working towards the same goal. We do not only have to overcome the language problem but also speak the same cultural international language which is very hard to learn and accept if our ideas differ.

Teachers as well as students who are new to an international work place have been formed and brought up in their own native cultures which reflect the way they actually behave towards one another. If you come from a culture with so-called high power distance you automatically teach or learn accordingly. Values like respect, obedience, supervision, control, ranking and grading, punishments and above all authority are important factors. Learning 'by fear' is another example, where the roles of the students and teachers are quite simple and clear. You either fail or succeed! The methodology is also often based on memorisation (multiple questions) and repetition rather than questioning and critical reasoning.

In cultures with low power distance (often in feminine business cultures) we encounter teachers and students who represent other ideas such as cooperation, team work, respect for the non-achievers, individual development according to ability, encouragement and tolerance. Teachers act more like colleagues and co-workers assisting in the learning process. Grading and ranking have less priority. Authority is not an important factor, but rather empathy and respect for each other as equal human beings, young or old. Other values are individual freedom to experiment and learn by trial and error which also involves less supervision and control. The goal is to make the students develop into responsible human beings who will learn to take

charge of their own lives. The methodology is rather that of critical thinking, analysing and understanding. Memorisation is not an important concept.

It is of course extremely important that we all understand the various cultural backgrounds we represent and respect each other and learn to cooperate across the cultural borders. By reasoning and learning from each other by the means of the academic learning process we will come far. Again, we must try to accept that all cultures have different ideas of how to acquire knowledge. In an international educational environment all these ideas meet and well handled, they will blend and hopefully multiply in the minds of our international students.

Time Concept
Many interculturalists point out that one of the more difficult cultural obstacles is in the way we look at time. Many expressions in Western cultures involve time. We talk about being on time, saving time, losing time, wasting time, time consumption, measured time and even killing time.

Punctuality is a sacred word in many cultures and not being or delivering on time could create immense irritation and bad business relations. Time is organised in time management calendars and measured in minutes for meetings and other activities. Our lives are organised according to a certain schedule that must not be disturbed or interfered with.

In other cultures time is of insignificant importance. Time is nothing that starts or ends but flows continually. What you cannot do today you will do tomorrow. Time can be used as a means of getting to know each other before the actual business contacts are established. Things must not be rushed but take time, and the initial contacts are made slowly and quietly in order to create mutual respect, harmony and trust.

Punctuality is not always considered important but something that very well could be disregarded if more important matters have turned up or somehow interfered with the actual plan for the day.

Whatever culture we represent we must try to adjust to the circumstances we face, since there is no way we can change the actual culture's rhythm and concept of time.

CONCLUSION

The best way to become a successful international co-worker is to approach the new culture with an open and curious mind without prejudice. We have to understand our own culture and its values and assumptions and then accurately profile the organisational and national culture of others. We have to reconcile ourselves with our new situation, accept the differences and be willing and eager to learn and even change our ideas accordingly if this is necessary.

Chapter Thirteen

SOCIAL LIFE

A move abroad will most likely bring about a drastic change in your social life, depending on the position to which you are assigned and the country to which you are moving. Work and social life are often connected. Your obligations will vary, but you can be assured that there might be a great difference between your previous social life and that abroad.

BEING IN FOCUS

You are sent out as a representative of your company and, in a sense, your country as well. You are a point of focus for your host and other nationals, as you represent another country and often a product or a service that is represented, sold or marketed in that particular country. In fact your identity is that of your company. In some countries, in particular developing ones, your family name might be exchanged for the brand name for which you work – e.g. Mr. and Mrs. Coca Cola!

You will be asked about your country and its political and social life, and you might be questioned and criticised. However, you will feel proud when your country is appreciated and noticed in the world. Try to be positive while living abroad, but avoid being too nationalistic. Don't forget to appreciate your host country and do not openly criticise the people or the social system, as this might be perceived as rude and disrespectful.

Your Company and its Products

Your company and its products or services are also represented through you, and you may notice that whenever problems arise with the product you market, sell or produce, people will come to you. You are the channel through which everything flows, regardless of whether you are the right person to approach. You must learn to smile and help the best you can, even if you feel wrongly accused at times.

This is in a way a 'doctor-patient syndrome' – in other words, a situation in which people feel compelled to discuss their medical history and new disorders as soon as they see a doctor.

On the other hand, you feel extremely proud of your company when its products are praised. You will become devoted to your company, as it represents, together with your country, your ultimate security and, as said above, your entire identity in the foreign country.

Invitations

Depending on your position, you might be invited to many different social gatherings as a representative of your company. Furthermore, it could be expected of you to hold dinners and other social activities for customers, associates or co-workers. The further away you are from home and the smaller the compatriot community, the higher you will climb on the social ladder – no matter what your status in the corporation at home.

HOMES – AN OPEN OR PRIVATE WORLD

The way we look at our homes differs tremendously from one culture to another. It has of course to do with our standard of living and economy but also our social life, customs and traditions.

In some countries there is a great emphasis on decorating our homes according to the various international trends often inspired by famous Hollywood movies or series that can been seen all over the world. The American influence in home decorating can be found in many countries today. Such a house has a large kitchen often connected with a family room or a media room and ample living quarters. This type of home is made for entertainment at home with lots of space for friends and guests.

The private world in the United States is in fact quite large insofar as opening up the home to strangers. You are even welcome to help yourself to a drink from the fridge in some homes. In many Western cultures, in particular the Scandinavian ones, we recognise the same type of homes in which many private activities take place.

On the other hand, the fact remains that most people living in large urban areas do not have the luxury of living in spacious homes but must make do with rather cramped living quarters. Home decorating does not have top priority and the home serves as a very private world for the family only. The private fridge is not available to each and everyone. Social activities instead take place in bars, pubs and restaurants and that is where all private entertaining also usually happens.

As an expatriate you usually upgrade your standard of living as you often have the possibility and economic support to choose a temporary home in a good area with houses and apartments of high standard.

Entertaining at Home

While living as an expatriate it might be expected of you to entertain business people, colleagues and other important persons in your home. It goes without saying that it is advisable to brush up on such trivial things as seating arrangements, table manners and other rules of etiquette before leaving. A good cookbook comes in handy as you might feel obliged to treat your host nationals with your own local dishes. Don't be afraid of using catering firms if you feel uncertain about what to serve.

DRESS CODE

The dress code varies from one occasion to another but on the whole, one could say that the international dress code on formal occasions are the same the world over. Men wear suits and women generally dresses and skirts instead of long pants, for example.

Informal social gatherings are usually very relaxed as far as dress code is concerned. Anything goes, from jeans and tee-shirts to smart attire. The individual taste is more important here. We can note, however, that in certain countries, for example Sweden, people tend to dress up more for social life. This is a contrast to some other countries where the dress code for social activities can be extremely relaxed.

In developing countries, you might be expected to wear something locally made and traditional, such as batik shirts for men in Indonesia and Malaysia, in order to show respect. Do not be surprised if the host nationals wear dark suits in order to show you respect.

TO HAVE AND HAVE NOT

In most Asian countries shoes are usually not worn among local people inside the home – a way to show respect. Here you will become used to seeing many bare feet of various shapes and sizes. Remember that in some Asian countries the sole of your foot must never be shown or pointed towards anybody as this is considered very rude.

If you are a guest in an Asian home, you must do what your host and hostess are doing. Follow the local customs.

In most Anglo-Saxon cultures as well as in many European countries it is considered a bit odd – sometimes even offensive – to take off one's shoes. Shoes are here considered part of your way of dressing and people feel very awkward walking around in socks or barefooted.

Again, do in Rome as the Romans do.

PUNCTUALITY

As discussed earlier we look at punctuality and time in many different ways and socially it is important to keep in mind that we adhere to the same rules. In many European countries we usually arrive on time – if not some minutes before – to a social function. In many other Western cultures we arrive 30 to 45 minutes late (France and the US for example) and in Latin and Asian countries you might not arrive at all – for many different reasons – Allah, supernatural powers, or plain traffic congestion.

INVITATION CARDS

It is recommended to send a written invitation to guests you invite to your home, also noting what the dress will be. It is best to be specific about what to wear to avoid embarrassing situations.

You usually have these alternatives:

- Casual: daily wear
- Informal: dark suit; short dress
- Formal: black tie, dinner jacket or smoking jacket; cock-tail/dinner dress
- Gala: black tie; long dress

RITUALS AND TRADITIONS

Remember that your customs may not be those of the host country. Check with your compatriots if it is advisable to bring flowers or gifts when visiting a person for the first time.

There might be flowers and even colours that we find beautiful but can represent something different in another country and culture. Read up on the country in question and avoid making initial mistakes. A bottle of fine brandy or whisky or a box of good chocolate are gifts that are appreciated in most countries in the world.

Gift giving is a very important tradition in many Asian countries. The presents must be beautifully wrapped and never opened in front of the person who offers the gift. The gift is handed over with both hands.

Small Talk

It is quite important to be able to master the skill of small talk, in other words to be able to carry on a conversation about fairly trivial things. Small talk could involve personal things like your family and your personal background, but most often it covers topics like travelling, hobbies and general impressions of the country. Try to avoid touchy subjects like politics, money matters and religion if you feel that you have strong, controversial opinions in these questions. Small talk is supposed to serve as an introduction to further acquaintance and it plays an important role in the start up of all business relations and new acquaintances.

Thank You Notes

In many countries it is regarded as polite to write a small note to your hosts, thanking them for a nice evening.

DEVELOPING COUNTRIES

Depending on the size of your compatriot community and the country in which you reside, your social engagements will vary. You will most likely be thrown into a social life that you have not experienced before.

There might be many receptions, dinners and cocktail parties at different embassies, various public places, clubs and hotels and, of course, private homes. You will meet politicians and diplomats. It is challenging, interesting and sometimes demanding, as you must be prepared to play many different and new social roles to which you might not be accustomed. Be natural and learn as you adjust to your new lifestyle.

ALCOHOL

With your new social obligations there is a good chance that you might be faced with an increased use of alcohol. Depending on your cultural (and genetic) background this will be of no problem at all or a fairly risky exposure. As said earlier, stress and hard work in combination with alcohol is not a good combination. It will only make matters worse.

Unfortunately, some people develop a relationship with alcohol during their assignments abroad that could be likened to an extended 'package tour syndrome' of several years. Daily life has to be constantly highlighted with drinks and entertaining and fairly normal, simple routines seem to fade away.

The accompanying spouse is at a great risk of developing an alcohol problem if she or he feels out of touch and isolated from the rest of the world. Drinking could serve as an escape or consolation from home-sickness and depression. A meaningful, active life is the best cure.

Danger Signals

Even if you feel that you are in control, you must be aware of the dangers of alcohol abuse and try to limit your intake if you must attend many cocktail parties and similar functions on a regular basis. You must learn to nourish a drink for a long time and keep track of the number of drinks you have had.

It is extremely easy to become used to a daily intake of alcohol which slowly and unnoticably increases by time. Alcoholism is very common among expatriates. Boredom, homesickness or stress and

tension will not be relieved by starting the day with a drink. According to some researchers and doctors specialising in alcohol, you are an alcoholic if you regularly drink alcohol once or twice a week. This is a controversial subject but it is important to keep an eye on oneself and one's partner.

Self Awareness

This is not intended to be a moralistic lesson in alcohol, but it is important to have self awareness. Give yourself a break for a couple of weeks now and then in order to clean your system and check the severity of your dependence upon alcohol.

Many marriages and relationships have been destroyed because of alcohol abuse. If you have a family it is even more important to remain a good role model to your children and give them the full support they need while growing up abroad in a foreign environment. It is not worthwhile risking your (and your family's) future on something that you really can live without.

Help

If you feel that you have problems, talk about them with someone you can trust and try to find help before it is too late. There are many excellent clinics and associations available nowadays to serve you – and remember that it is not shameful to be an alcoholic. You will be treated as someone who is suffering from any other disease. It is not incurable.

NEW FRIENDS

Through an active social life you will get to know many new people from various parts of the world since you move around in an international community. You will often develop long lasting friendship which will make you feel more at home in your new country and once you move you will find that you have friends you can visit the world all over. This creates international bonds that you and your family can enjoy for the rest of your life.

Making friends takes some effort but once you feel that you have established good contacts, it is well worth cultivating this relationship in order to keep your new friends.

Chapter Fourteen

THE JEKYLL & HYDE SYNDROME

ROLE PLAYING

The process of changing identities when living in two cultures is like playing two roles that sometimes become conflicting. Your native role feels of course natural and clear as long as you play it at home, but as you learn to act in your new culture you gradually distance yourself from that familiar role.

This has to do with visible things like behaviour, body language, gestures, the way you dress but also how you express yourself. You adapt and become influenced by your new surroundings. This is even more evident in your accompanying children who have a stronger sense of belonging to a group and to become accepted by their peers. Everybody goes through a slow transformation without noticing it. The new culture becomes contagious in fact.

CHANGING VALUES

Mentally you change also. New values are added and some old ones are discarded. You might have been brought up with rather fixed ideas – some very good and well worth preserving – that concern your general outlook on life and on people. Many of your fundamental ideas will be tested and tried and, in fact, even altered which eventually might make you foreign in your own country.

It can also involve practical things like your general view on safety and security for example – important concepts in well regulated countries. You might have been taught that it is important to keep to the speed limits and use the safety belt when going by car, or wear a safety helmet when riding a motorbike in order to protect yourself (and avoid fines). When you are dropped into a culture where no one seems to worry about personal safety, you experience yourself as a peculiar outsider and might be tempted to forget what you know is right.

Another example is drinking and driving which in many cultures is an absolute taboo compared to countries with a liberal view on alcohol behind the wheel. In spite of the fact that you know that the combination of driving and drinking is dangerous, you might reject what you once have learnt to respect.

THE GOOD AND THE EVIL

In general it seems to be easy to forget the rigid laws that have been made for our own protection. Many quickly adopt the individual right to choose, even if it is a bad choice. This is where the 'Dr. Jekyll and Mr. Hyde syndrome' comes into effect, since many are tempted to live life a bit more dangerously even if they feel that it is wrong.

It goes without saying that people, coming from a culture with a liberal view on these matters or with very few civil laws, find it at first very frustrating to adjust to a well disciplined society. They might feel stripped of their personal integrity. Mr. Hyde has a hard time becoming the well behaved Dr. Jekyll. The learning process could in fact be very costly to Mr. Hyde if he does not obey the laws quickly.

THE UNTOUCHABLES

When living in a foreign country, you sometimes have a feeling that you do not actually belong anywhere. Your own norms and values feel distant. You do not take active part in your own country's daily life, and thus feel disengaged. You cannot either take part in your host country's political life, as you are an outsider. This can lead to the illusion that you are somehow untouchable. You do not know all the laws and regulations of the new country and, as you do not feel part of it, you create your own laws and rules.

Because you feel far from the reach of your own society, you experience a lawlessness that can make you behave in many strange ways and take unnecessary risks.

ISOLATION AND CENSORSHIP

You are beyond reach in a cultural sense as well, sometimes because of difficulties in communication and a lack of common cultural background with the host nationals. You might not be able to follow the news or obtain good information in newspapers and magazines. In some countries, you are even withheld information, as the press is censored. Generally, you will note that every country reflects the standards and beliefs of the political viewpoints of that country, some of which will be completely contrary to those you have.

YOUR OWN LAWS

In creating your own standards and laws, you will notice that many of these even conflict with those of your own country, but somehow you feel that you do not have to worry about the consequences. You might believe that you have 'political immunity' and feel out of reach. Beware – this is just an illusion.

This 'lawlessness' can also be reflected in your not showing respect for the laws and practices (often religious) of the host country. Remember that many of your own values are totally new to your foreign country and might be perceived as offensive and wrong. In some countries, you must dress in a certain way. It might not be appropriate to wear Western clothes which we find fully decent and acceptable. Women might be expected to cover themselves when out in public. We must show our host nationals respect, whether we like it or not.

The way we look at exposing our bodies differs from one culture to another. Topless sunbathing might be fully accepted in most European countries while in other countries, including many states in the United States, not even a baby girl is allowed to use a topless bikini.

DRUGS AND ALCOHOL

Use of alcohol and drugs that might be accepted in one country could be considered a criminal offence in another. If you are caught handling drugs in Malaysia or Singapore, for example, you will be sentenced to death. Be extremely careful when travelling and do not leave unattended baggage anywhere. You might become a drug courier without even knowing about it, but you will bear the consequences.

NO 'NO MAN'S LAND'

We must tread carefully in our new country and watch our step. There is of course no such thing as a 'No Man's Land' even if we would like to create one. We must be aware of the fact that the laws of the country in which we live are applicable to us as well and, in many instances, they can hurt us more than we are able to comprehend.

Chapter Fifteen

SAFETY ABROAD

A DANGEROUS WORLD

Being an expatriate, you will definitely expose yourself to greater danger than a non-travelling citizen of your country does. Not only do you travel frequently, and often to faraway destinations, but you might also settle in countries in which the political situation is quite unstable.

Many expatriates working for their governments and other institutions or international companies have risked their own and their families' lives in placing themselves in the middle of a political uprising. Some have been brutalised, hijacked, kidnapped and even killed.

The only comfort to be gotten from this situation is learning to manage living through difficult situations, however hopeless they may seem, and emerging as a stronger human being. We are able to adapt to many strange circumstances. It is certain that many nerve wracking experiences will be remembered forever, and some will haunt you for the rest of your life.

This is the price you must pay and the risk that must be taken when accepting an assignment abroad. You should be aware that this insecurity will hang over you and your family wherever you travel.

TERRORISM

> ... term usually applied to organised acts or threats of violence to intimidate opponents or to publicise grievances. It frequently involves bombing, kidnapping, airplane hijacking, the taking of hostages and assassination.
>
> Political terrorism may be part of a government campaign to eliminate the opposition, or it may be part of a revolutionary effort to overthrow a regime, a common tactic in guerilla warfare.
>
> —*The Concise Columbia Encyclopedia*

In this day and age, we have grown accustomed to living under the threat of terrorism, as cruel and incomprehensible as it must have been in the time that this term was created during the French Revolution.

The problem seems to increase with the years and the underlying political reasons vary. The terrorist groups taking part in these activities are extremely dangerous and fanatical, aiming at completely innocent civilians that usually have nothing to do with the act of violence. They are sacrificed in the name of vengeance and hatred. Terrorists must be taken very seriously. Suicidal attacks are the most common and they happen often without a forewarning. We can usually not protect ourselves from these attacks.

Terrorism is a reality today, and we seem to have difficulties accepting that these acts happen when we least expect them. Our societies are extremely vulnerable and innocent people are easy targets in urban areas, in particular commuters on buses, trains and other mass transit communication, but also on international airlines. There is no way we can foresee or avoid being where the deed is going to take place. It is a matter of circumstance and unfortunate timing or extremely bad luck.

Proper Proportions

One must try, however, to put terrorism in proportion to all the other dangers we must face in this world. We must also hope that diplomatic and political efforts will be successful in stopping these insanities. The relaxation of tension between the superpowers and the ambition among our world leaders to solve political crises diplomatically might help to solve many of the basically religious conflicts in the world.

Seen from another perspective, we must realise that car accidents alone take a much larger death toll annually than all international terrorist actions together. Approximately 50,000 people are killed, in the United States alone every year in car accidents. That makes terrorist actions seem at least a little less significant.

Be Prepared

If you reside in a country threatened by terrorism or political uprising, you will be advised by the your embassy or consulate as to where to go in case of emergency. They will supply you with all necessary information.

- Always keep your personal documents and other important papers in a folder that is easy to bring in case you must leave quickly.

- Make sure that you have a medical survival kit handy in case you should need it.

- Be prepared for an eventual evacuation and make sure you know what to do and where to go in order to avoid panic. Avoid alcohol or other drugs.

- Always respect curfews.

- Try to listen to a shortwave radio and the BBC World Service or Voice of America.

- If you think you can get help from a local person, be extremely careful when making contact in order to avoid unnecessary risks.

Hijacking

If you are unfortunate enough to travel on a plane that is being hijacked you must try to keep your nerves under control. There is no reason to try to provoke a hijacker or for that matter try to act heroically. Do as you are told. These terrorists have one goal in mind and that is to have the world pay attention to what they have to say. Listen and do not argue with them. Stay in your seat and always ask for permission to leave if you need to go to the lavatory. Do not surprise them as this might cause them to act violently.

Only the cabin crew should negotiate with these terrorists, as they are responsible for your security. They should be well prepared to handle hijackers or other emergencies.

Kidnapping

In certain countries criminals or political activists specialise in the taking of hostages or kidnapping. This can happen in any country but we might experience a greater risk when living in politically unstable or poor countries.

In communities where there are very few expatriates, they are more in focus, not only because they look different but also often live in the fashionable, expensive areas and often represent money and power (sometimes even a superpower). This attracts criminals who need cash.

But kidnapping can also have other reasons – not the least political ones – where a small group of terrorists want the world to pay attention to their particular problem.

Embassy representatives are usually trained to handle these situations and one should try to avoid provoking these criminals since they seldom shy away from violence. Do as you are being told. Negotiations and exhausting discussions seem to be the only means of reaching a solution. The paying of ransom is not always considered the best alternative in spite of the fact that a person's life could be at stake.

If you live in an area known for this type of personal threat, you must see to it that you and your family are properly guarded and protected. Try to avoid any types of daily routines that run on schedule, if possible, and do not travel the same routes to your work place every day. Be watchful and pay attention to unfamiliar persons hanging around your workplace or your home.

THIEVES, ROBBERS AND PICKPOCKETS

Wherever we go today we risk losing our wallets, purses or other valuables. There are of course certain international 'waterholes' for small criminals like these. We usually find them in populated areas where people stressfully change one means of transportation to another – airlines, trains, boats, buses or subways. They can operate quite anonymously in these places and their victims are usually concentrating on being on time, finding the right gate or making new contacts.

We also find thieves operating in hotel lobbies and restaurants and of course large department stores and markets. Hang on to your handbag and keep your wallet out of reach. Try to avoid large crowds

131

if possible, although this is sometimes simply not an option. Do not expose your gold chains and expensive watches, but keep a low profile.

In case you lose your handbag or wallet and maybe credit cards and other important documents, see to it that you have a backup at home with photocopies of all your papers and private ID-cards. Have a handy telephone list to all your bank contacts and credit card companies, so that you can cancel your accounts at once. Do not forget to notify the police and your insurance company.

ARMED ROBBERIES

In many large international urban areas armed robberies seem to be on the increase. The weapons used are often knives and guns. Take a desperate robber very seriously. Try to keep yourself calm. Hand over what is demanded of you. Do not try to discuss or argue with the person since he or she is completely unpredictable.

DRIVING IN UNFAMILIAR AREAS

Before driving into a new area of a large city, for example, orientate yourself and study a map. Locate exits and road numbers, gas stations and try to find a police station. Use the main roads and avoid unknown short-cuts. Avoid driving at night time until you have learnt to find your way around.

Other general rules are:
- Never give lifts to hitchhikers.
- Lock your car doors when driving in big city traffic.
- Never place your briefcase or handbag visibly on the front seat.
- Never leave anything of value in your car.

FEAR

After having read the above you might ask yourself if it is really worthwhile moving to a country that feels insecure and unstable.

Remember that things usually sound worse when listed as above. This is just written to make you prepared in the unlikely event you will experience anything similar.

It was once said by President Franklin D Roosevelt that the only fear we should fear, is fear itself. This can be applied to many of our own difficult situations. We must face the dangers in the world, avoid irrational fear and panic and try to stay calm. By doing so, we will become psychologically stronger and perhaps less vulnerable as well.

Another famous US president, Thomas Jefferson, said: "How much pain the evils have cost us that never happened." This is both very true and comforting to remember when we feel worried and insecure.

Chapter Sixteen

HOME LEAVE

Most people on longer assignments abroad are given home leave once a year. This is usually taken during the summer months in Europe and the US. Australians and New Zealanders prefer taking an extended vacation during Christmas when the weather is warm and pleasant. Whenever you go, you will find that this is a wonderful and necessary way of returning to your 'roots' and catching up with friends and relatives.

RECONNECTION

It is an invaluable experience to return home regularly, particularly for accompanying children, as they will be able to practice their native language more freely and reconnect with their country.

As mentioned earlier, it is quite important to return to the same home base every year and, if possible, to the same place where the children have grown up. They will meet their old friends and be able to share their adventures with them. At the same time, they will learn what has happened during the year they have been away. There is a risk that they will have feelings of alienation at first and not feel like part of the group that they have left. However, given time, they will soon feel at home again.

It is wise to return to the same physical place as this will prevent your children from feeling rootless and like outsiders in their own environment. Having two home countries will split your children to some extent, and they will have dual loyalties as long as you are living abroad. They seem, however, to be able to adjust fairly quickly to their different lifestyles.

ALIENS

Some kind of 'culture crash' will often follow upon your return home after a year abroad. Much has changed during that year and, in the beginning, you feel like a foreigner – somehow, you do not fit in.

You are not up to date on the latest news. You are forced to ask stupid questions, such as the price of postage. There might be new devices or new ways of doing things that are unfamiliar to you and difficult to understand. There are new rules and regulations that you have missed. You make a strange impression, as you do not speak with an accent or look foreign and out of place. People treat you with a certain suspicion, and you feel hesitant as to whether to explain your 'strange' behaviour. Try to relearn quickly and do not make too much of an issue of it.

SLIPPING AWAY

If your assignment lasts for an extended period of time, you will gradually slip away from some of your friends because you do not have as much in common any more. You grow apart and develop in different directions. This is especially the case with accompanying children who have left their friends during a very crucial period in their lives. Many believe that you make your lifetime friends during your school years.

The above dilemma is difficult to solve but, in order to avoid a permanent feeling of alienation among these expatriated families, the assignment abroad should be restricted to a maximum of four to five years. It is important to return home and 'recharge the batteries,' become updated and on a par with all your compatriots. Otherwise, there is a great risk that you will wind up in an international vacuum and slip away from your own roots. The longer the stay abroad, the harder the return home.

HEALTH CHECK-UP

When on home leave, it is of utmost importance to have a thorough health checkup and a visit to the dentist, especially when living in developing countries. Immunisations must be updated as well.

Tropical Countries and Health

Living in a tropical country, you are at a greater risk in terms of health, as there are so many more diseases that can develop slowly such as tuberculosis, malaria, amoebas and other intestinal disorders. Some of these infections do not cause any significant problems until they have developed into a more complicated stage and will naturally then be more difficult to cure. You might have vitamin deficiencies that you are not aware of until you experience severe symptoms. It is advisable to have your doctor check your levels of vitamin B12 and folic acid. If these indicate a decrease, it could be a sign of a disorder called Tropical Sprue. A quick checkup and some blood tests will verify that you are healthy.

A MUCH LONGED-FOR TIME

You will find that your home leave will be a much longed-for and necessary yearly break in your foreign assignment, as it will make you feel a part of your country again.

The most important part is of course to be able to see your family and your close friends again. Never, ever lose contact with your near and dear since they have your affection and love but also represent your cultural background and security. When things go roughly you will always return to your roots – see to it that you maintain your connections with them – there is no place like home!

Chapter Seventeen

RELOCATION AND REPATRIATION

> Considering this in a reasonable way, it must be said, if
> only in a whisper, that experience is better than theory.
>   —Amerigo Vespucci (1501)

When your assignment is completed and you face the trauma of
breaking away from a country and a home that has become precious
to you, you will undoubtedly experience a certain amount of strain
and stress. There will be moments of sadness and despair when facing
the last goodbye to your borrowed yet so familiar home in a foreign
country.

Leaving a Good Job

You have had an interesting job and made many new contacts, you
have learned (hopefully) to cooperate with your host nationals, you
have developed and matured with your new assignment and might
even have grown attached to your workplace.

Your spouse has also become an important part of your work life, giving you support and help in difficult times. She has been integrated into your corporative culture much more actively than in your home country. She will also face a feeling of loss for your colleagues and work as well as her own spheres of activity.

Leaving Friends

You must leave your new friends who have become very dear to you. In fact, many have become your pseudo-relatives. Your children will leave classmates, teachers and friends and a school that, at its best, has taught them many new things.

Leaving a Developing Country

If you leave a developing country, you must also part from your household staff, who have become part of your family and to whom you have grown very attached. Your pets might also have to stay behind, to the great sadness of you and your children.

Dear Memories

It is said that a meaningful goodbye gives you a creative hello. You must not leave any loose ends but feel mentally prepared for this breakup. It is necessary to see all the friends you are leaving behind and say a last goodbye. Visit some of your favourite places and give yourself time to say goodbye to them too. Go slowly as you leave.

Part of your heart will stay in the country forever and you will cherish your memories for a long time to come.

Our Human Mind

However, it seems as if our human minds are made to face and help us overcome many critical situations. Somehow you manage to unpack all your positive feelings and expectations regarding a new life at home. You remember the people and things you have missed, although you have perhaps suppressed the feelings while living abroad. Your native country is seen in a new light. You feel hopeful and happy in returning.

While living abroad, you might have held back certain feelings and mentally turned away from phenomena in the society that you were not able to accept. These feelings can now be unleashed and help you to see your foreign country in a different light also.

The mechanism is quite simple. In order to be able to adapt to a society, you must censor certain things while living there. As said earlier, this is part of the culture shock, as you cannot use all of your own cultural values in a foreign country. It seems, however, to be of help to release all the hidden native values, once you are ready to leave. That will make you ready to face your repatriation.

A RE-ENTRY SHOCK

You might think that coming back to your own country should not be very problematic. You know the language and the culture, and you probably have your home, friends and relatives waiting for you. You might return to a new and more challenging job and your former colleagues are expecting you back.

There are, however, many reasons for a readjustment crisis. Below is a list of those which are most common. It will hopefully serve to sharpen your awareness and help prepare for a successful re-entry. If you are ready for some of these challenges you will be able to tackle them as you face them. If you are fortunate enough to have a smooth homecoming be grateful because most returning expatriates have a fairly rough time before settling at home again.

- A changed social and cultural lifestyle
- A changed economy
- Job shock or job shrink
- Problems with housing

- Problems with children's education
- The accompanying spouse's readjustment
- The family's readjustment

A TIME OF CHANGE

You have definitely changed while living abroad. You have acquired many new cultural values, discovered a new world outside your own country and maybe travelled to many exciting places. You have gotten a bird's eye view of the world, and your country or home state might appear very small and your compatriots even narrow-minded.

The values you grew up with have been diversified and you understand that there is more than one side to a coin. You might feel that the people you meet are provincial and not very interested in any of your international experiences.

A FOREIGN NATIVE COUNTRY

The country you left some years ago is not the same. Many changes have taken place. People have changed and their lives have sometimes taken turns which you have not been a part of.

Your country keeps developing socially and politically. Incidents have happened that you have not experienced personally. Reading about them or watching the news from far away does not give you a proper appreciation.

You are an outsider and have a couple of years' 'parenthesis' in your native country's life. You lack the common denominators to which people refer when talking about the past years.

YOUR FOREIGN EXPERIENCE

You will also note that people do not generally care about your international life or work experience abroad. You might feel unappreciated by your colleagues and sometimes unwanted. You represent

141

'the unknown' to many and, as you feel foreign in your attitudes, many turn away from you. It is extremely difficult for a native who has never left his culture to see things through your 'foreign' eyes. The underlying reasons are difficult to grasp and accept, because you feel you have so much to share. We may often suspect that such sentiments as jealousy, rivalry or enviousness play a role – or maybe it is just plain ignorance. Seek comfort among your friends and colleagues who have previous experience from life abroad.

A FAMILY AFFAIR

Your family will face the same problems. Your children are not updated about the latest pop, movie and sport stars, the local pop music and movies. They might dress and look different. They might be behind in their schoolwork, they can have language problems and encounter teachers who do not understand that they must deal with a student/child who sounds and acts like a native, but does not have the same frames of reference as his classmates. These children return with a new set of social norms and must be given time and support to fit into their new school situation.

Unfortunately, they are expected to conform to the group right away, without making too much fuss. They are not given the extra care and attention which is provided to many immigrants, in spite of the fact that they are 'immigrants' themselves, often with a span of several years away from home.

THE SPOUSE

Your accompanying spouse will usually have a hard time readjusting, particularly if the stay abroad has been enjoyable. She is also the last one to become settled as she generally must see to it first that the home is organised and the family in place.

If she has been active professionally before the assignment abroad, she must find a new job and she might feel out of touch and behind in things.

Her feeling of isolation and alienation might dominate for some time, particularly if it is common that women work and are very active outside of home; in certain countries housewives have become a rarity.

A Foreign Spouse

As said earlier, many people who began as singles abroad return home with a spouse and a new family. International and intercultural/racial marriages experience much more pressure when relocated. An adjustment to a new lifestyle and culture will be time consuming and frustrating. This, in combination with the learning of, for example, a new language, will involve many problems and demand much patience and understanding from all concerned.

It is of utmost importance to be prepared for a severe culture shock because life at home is not similar to an international lifestyle, full of excitement and joy. If you return to a society which is traditionally very homogeneous you might encounter people who are prejudiced and suspicious of strangers.

Mixed relationships are readily accepted in many cultures, in particular if there are no language problems or other difficulties like markedly different physical characteristics. If you return to a home country, however, that is very foreign to your new spouse reality can become fairly harsh.

It is also worthwhile to mention that life usually changes drastically, both economically and socially, when adjusting at home. It has been said that home is where you worry about money. It is easier for some reason to spend money when it is a foreign currency. The native country's money is perceived as being more valuable and important.

The most evident difference is, however, that the international flair is gone.

A SECOND LANGUAGE

If needed, a language course will help your foreign spouse to be better prepared for a good start in your native culture. It is advisable to start training in your home language while living abroad, as this will eliminate a huge problem upon your return. The foreign partner will be able to communicate right away, and the feeling of isolation will not be as great.

THE FOUR STAGES OF RE-ENTRY SHOCK

The re-entry shock is very similar to that of the culture shock described earlier. It is often experienced as something more dramatic than the foreign shock, because it is not expected. It is ironic that the better the stay abroad, the more severe the culture shock at return. You will find that an assimilation to the native culture can take up to two years. Again, it is necessary to approach the re-entry and your native culture with a positive attitude and try to understand your reactions. Your own culture can feel very alien and threatening for some time.

Initially, you feel very happy about being back home again. Your country feels almost exotic as you rediscover all the familiar but almost forgotten facets of living at home. Your old, but still new home provides a welcoming atmosphere. You feel like a tourist in your own country!

Secondly, you might pass into a stage of irritation, anger, hopelessness and a feeling of wanting to leave again, because your new values make you re-evaluate your lifestyle. (Note: This is a stage during which many have given up and returned to their foreign country or accepted another foreign assignment.) This period has to be tackled with perseverance and a good fighting spirit, because the outcome is going to be positive.

The third stage is a time when you slowly adjust to your country again, as the turning point has been reached and you recover from all the frustration you have felt.

The last and fourth stage is when you feel adapted and adjusted again. Your roots start to grow and you and your family feel at home again. However, your original values have changed and there will always be phenomena in your native culture that will seem strange and unacceptable. Your international life has given you a new perspective and outlook. You will also better appreciate and understand your native country and accept it for what it is.

Once you have experienced these feelings you will be able to remember the time you have spent abroad without feeling sad or frustrated. You begin to function in society again, wanting to get involved and sharing your knowledge with others.

If you return to your 'foreign' country one day, you will experience it from a distance and treat the time spent there as part of a great adventure which gave you and your family the wonderful possibility of living a different life.

OVERKILL IN COMMUNICATION

Upon your return home, many of your friends and relatives will be bored to death hearing about your international experience. A good piece of advice is to hold back your wish to share your memories until you feel they are ready for it. Do not force yourself upon them. Hopefully, they will understand that there is a great need for you to share what you have lived through. On the other hand, do not close yourself up. This will not do you any good in the long run. Sometimes it is easier to reach out to find understanding and a listening ear by sharing your feelings. That way, your listeners do not perceive what you say as bragging.

A FINAL NOTE

Remember, that in spite of all the many turns and difficulties you might undergo, you are the winner and not the loser. Your life abroad has allowed you to gain tremendous experience – both in work and life – and it has given you and your family new dimensions and an international understanding that is beyond reach for most people.

It is said that we human beings can be divided into two groups: farmers and hunters. The farmers stay where they were born and the hunters leave.

Many expatriates can be likened to the hunters, with a longing for open spaces, a constant wish to discover new territories and a curiosity to find out what is beyond the next mountain. This is a character trait that might always remain, even in a happily repatriated person.

1988

Take a little trip through time
I see the pictures getting clearer
A million faces in the mirror
I stop awhile and turn around
Seeing memories my mind has found
Each impression now getting stronger
Freeze the image just a little bit longer
Summers going fast
And nights growing colder
Everybody is getting older and older
Don't let it all just slip away
Like a coin in a wishing well
I have a moment to spare
To take a little trip through time
Taking me – a little trip through time
I try to take the sheet away
Hiding thoughts of yesterday
I feel the warmth upon my face
An old place left another trace
Long ago
I hear the laughter of an old friend
Never knowing then it had to end

—Fredrik Rabe (17 years)

THE AUTHOR

Monica A. Rabe was raised in the small town of Falköping, east of Götburg, in Sweden. She has lived for over fourteen years, during three separate intervals, with her husband and four children in South East Asia and North America, and has travelled extensively all over the world.

Monica has had a number of different jobs while living abroad, in banking, travel agencies, offices and schools. She has also had an import/export business in the fashion industry.

Although a high school teacher by profession (M.A. in Swedish and English), she is now working as an international consultant and lecturer preparing families and individuals for international living. She is also part owner of a relocation company in Sweden.

Monica Rabe has also written *Living and Working in Sweden*, *Kulturella Glasögon – med svensk syn utomlands* and translated Dr. Robert Sinclair's book *Utlandshälsovård (Health Care Abroad)* into English.

INDEX

adjusting 58, 123–126
  changing values 124
  local laws 125
  resisting temptation 124
alcohol 100, 120–121, 126
  avoiding problems 120

business culture 104, 108–110
  Confucian Dynamism 110
  masculine and feminine 108
  power distance 108
  uncertainty avoidance 109

communication 70–75
  body language 73, 123
  cross cultural 72
  dos and don'ts 73
  forms of address 75
  taboos 74
cultural differences 105–106,
    112
  time and punctuality 112, 118
culture, defining 12–18
culture shock 59, 62–64
  stages 59, 60–61

dating 87, 90
domestic help 42–43, 97
driving 57
drugs 100–102, 126

family
  accompanying spouse 19–20,
    66, 94, 96, 142
  children 19, 21, 33–34, 39–
    40, 63, 67, 76, 78–81, 85,
    98, 142
    education 30, 39, 76–83
    safety 55
    teenagers 99, 103
  depression 97
  home life 95
  leaving the country 139
  marriage and relationships 21,
    93
    divorce 94
  parents and grandparents 21
  pets 36

gender roles 86–87, 90, 110

health 22, 24, 30, 35, 43, 46,
    48–49, 52, 136
  check-ups 136
  dental 30
  diseases and infections 45–48
  emergencies 52
  HIV/AIDS 30, 45, 91
  malaria 47
  private health card 36
  vaccination 30
Hofstede, Geert 107

home country
  national pride 63
  staying in touch 20
home leave 31, 134–137
  reconnection 134
host country 54
housing 38–41, 45, 116
  agents 38
  decorating 116
  utilities 42

intercultural teaching 111
intercultural understanding 107

language 29, 65–69, 84–85, 143
  English 66
    British or American 68
  ESL 81
  learning 66
  local slang 67
loneliness 88, 91

moving 28–36
  furniture 32
  packing 31
  storage 26, 34

overseas marriages 89

prostitution 91

refugees 62
returning home 138–146
  re-entry shock 140, 144

rituals and traditions 118

security 55, 127–133
  personal safety 56, 129
    driving 132
    kidnapping 130
  pickpockets 131
  terrorism 128–129
  hijacking 130
shopping 52–53
  bargaining 53
  local markets 53
social life 114–122
  dress 117
  entertaining 116
  invitations 115
  small talk 119
social systems 51
stress 64

working abroad
  family and work 94
  goals and needs 20
  leaving 138
  personal identity 115
  preparation 19,–25, 104
  stress 64

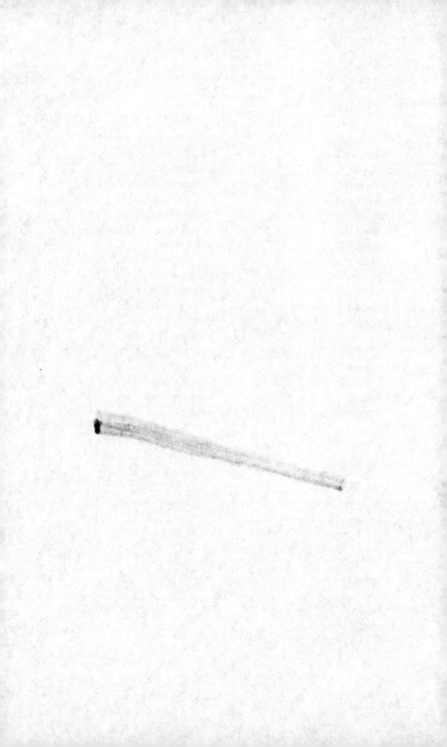